Instructions for the Training of Divisions for Offensive Action. Reprint from Pamphlet Issued by the British General Staff, War Office, December, 1916

Great Britain. War Office. General Staff

INSTRUCTIONS FOR THE
TRAINING OF DIVISIONS
FOR
OFFENSIVE ACTION

REPRINT FROM PAMPHLET ISSUED BY
BRITISH GENERAL STAFF, WAR OFFICE
DECEMBER, 1916

———

WASHINGTON
GOVERNMENT PRINTING OFFICE
1917

U
161

1917

WAR DEPARTMENT.
Document No. 623.
Office of The Adjutant General.

(2)

WAR DEPARTMENT,
WASHINGTON, *July 5, 1917.*

The following instructions of the British on the training of divisions for offensive action are published for the information of all concerned.

[062.11, A. G. O.]

BY ORDER OF THE SECRETARY OF WAR.

TASKER H. BLISS,
Major General, Acting Chief of Staff.

OFFICIAL:

H. P. McCAIN,
The Adjutant General.

(3)

CONTENTS.

(5)

6

INTRODUCTION.

1. All training behind the line must be specially directed toward offensive action.

2. The operations for which our troops must be prepared and trained are:

(*a*) The initial attack against a well-organized and long-established position.

(*b*) Attacks against improvised defenses following on successful assaults on the enemy's original main positions.

(*c*) Open warfare.

3. An essential difference between these three forms of operation is the time available for reconnaissance and preparation.

In (*a*) ample time should be available for reconnaissance and preparation. Plans must be thought out, all developments foreseen, and every detail worked out beforehand most minutely and carefully.

The whole operation can be rehearsed over an exact replica of the trenches to be assaulted, until every individual knows his task thoroughly and can be trusted to carry it through, even if his leaders become casualties.

In (*b*) and (*c*) time is a most important factor; the results gained as a consequence of successful assaults on the enemy's prepared systems of defense will depend very much on the rapidity with which the first successes can be followed up.

To meet this requirement it is necessary that commanders of all grades shall be trained to grasp quickly the essential features of a tactical situation and to issue orders dealing with it. It is equally important that the troops shall be capable of putting these orders, under such conditions, into immediate execution.

The training of the armies we have now in the field has been almost entirely in methodical trench warfare, and thorough knowledge and skill in this is required to insure success in the first assaults on the enemy's position. But much more is required. All ranks must understand that such methodical procedure is designed to meet special conditions and that to develop

(7)

successfully they must be capable of following it up with rapidity and skill.

The time available to prepare for attacks on improvised lines of defense lying immediately behind the enemy's original main positions must depend on circumstances and on the strength of the defenses to be assaulted. As a general principle the more rapidly such attacks can be launched and carried through the better.

In such cases reconnaissance must be rapid, the plan must be on broad lines, simple and straightforward, and the operation orders will be brief. It will not be possible to provide for every detail.

The following instructions apply specially to training for methodical attacks on prepared positions. Training for open warfare will be carried out on the principles laid down in Field Service Regulations and the Training Manuals.

4. The preparatory measures for an attack from trenches and the preliminary arrangements required are laid down in the memorandum "Preparatory Measures to be Taken by Armies and Corps before Undertaking Operations on a Large Scale." (O. B. 1207, dated 2/2/16.)

A summary of the chief points in this memorandum, which apply particularly to divisions, is given in Appendix A.

In the case of an original attack against a long-established position, divisions should, if possible, take over that portion of the line from which their assault will be delivered at least 10 days before the date fixed for the attack, in order to enable all ranks of the division to become thoroughly acquainted with the ground and to give time for the completion of any final preparations which may not have been finished by the previous occupants of the line. Wherever possible assaulting divisions should be allowed to make all their own preparations and should be in occupation of their sector for a sufficiently long time to enable them to do so.

In the case of attacks against improvised lines, divisions should take over their portion of the line as early as possible in order to give them time for preparation.

5. The time available for training as complete divisions or brigades behind the line will not usually permit of individual training being carried out during these periods. This must be done while in the line.

If possible, double the establishment of specialists, i. e., scouts, observers, snipers, signalers, stretcher bearers, and in the case of Lewis gun detachments treble the establishment should be trained.

In addition all ranks of the infantry and pioneers should have thrown live grenades and should, if possible, know how to fire the Lewis gun.

6. On arrival in the training area a few days should be spent in reorganization and tightening up discipline, which is liable to suffer from a prolonged spell of trench work.

Sections, platoons, and companies must be properly organized under their own leaders, and these leaders must be practiced in handling their commands, and must train them and train with them on all occasions.

The organization of bombers, Lewis gun detachments, scouts, observers, snipers, signalers, stretcher bearers, and runners must be taken in hand.

The morale of the unit must be improved by attention to saluting, turn out, clothing, and by close-order drill.

7. The training ground requires careful preparation.

The trench system to be attacked must be laid out on the training ground to scale, and the actual trenches dug to a depth of 1 foot at least.

All enemy trenches which are included in the divisional task, as also the next position in rear, should be marked out, although the latter need only be flagged.

Similarly our own front system and communication trenches, back as far as the intermediate line, should be marked out and dug.

Where time does not permit of trenches being dug, they must be marked out with tracing tape and flags, although this is not so satisfactory as practicing over actual trenches.

8. The troops must be practiced over the model trenches until every man knows exactly what he has to do.

Training must commence with platoons and companies working independently, and progress gradually till brigades and even the whole division have carried out the operation as a complete unit.

Where time for training is short, commanders must insure that each battalion is thoroughly trained before attempting to carry out practices with larger formations.

9. In order to develop initiative and a capacity for maneuver, umpires must always be employed to create a variety of tactical situations.

Tactical exercises over the model trenches with leaders only, both officers and N.C.O.'s, can be usefully employed.

Exercises in billets, with trench maps and air photographs of the trenches to be attacked, enable tactical problems to be set and discussed; these problems can be worked out in practice with the troops next day on the ground.

10. The points dealt with in the subsequent paragraphs are those to which attention should be chiefly devoted during training.

They apply to both the original attack against a well-established line and to the attack against improvised lines behind the main position.

In each case attention is drawn to any modification required by either class of operation.

INSTRUCTIONS FOR THE TRAINING OF DIVISIONS FOR OFFENSIVE ACTION.

I. Issue of Orders by Divisional and Brigade Commanders.

1. The divisional commander, having been allotted his task by the corps and informed generally of the Artillery plan, and after having carried out the necessary reconnaissance, forms his own plan, which will include the task to be carried out by each body of infantry, generally how each body is to be disposed prior to the assault, and his general intentions as to the action of his reserve.

2. As soon as this plan has been approved by the corps commander, it is issued immediately in the form of instructions to subordinate commanders, together with any information available as to the action of the divisions on either flank.

This is the warning order and the earlier it is issued the more time will be available for subordinate commanders to make their plans and preparations and to issue instructions to their subordinates.

3. The divisional staff then work out the necessary details to give effect to the plan and issue them in a series of " Instructions " as and when they have been worked out.

Copies of all divisional instructions should be sent to all recipients of operation orders as laid down in divisional standing orders and also to corps headquarters, corps artillery, corps heavy artillery, all divisional artilleries detailed by the corps to support the division, corps machine-gun officer, R.F.C. squadron working with the corps and divisions on either flank.

4. The points which require to be dealt with in these instructions and the order in which they should normally be issued are as follows :

(*a*) Work required to organize our own trenches for the attack, including the construction of observation and command posts.

(*b*) Signal communications.

(11)

(*c*) Assembly areas and allotment of trenches for "In" and "Out" communication.

(*d*) Use of gas and smoke and arrangements for installing former.

(*e*) Formation of store, ration, and water dumps and arrangements for keeping them filled.

(*f*) Medical arrangements.

(*g*) Fighting kit, including flares, rockets, grenades, etc., to be carried; arrangements for storing packs; distinguishing marks.

(*h*) Police arrangements for stragglers' posts.

(*i*) Number of officers, N.C.O.'s, and specialists to accompany assaulting battalions. Appointments of understudies for staff and nomination of officers to command in the event of casualties.

(*j*) Artillery plan, including preliminary bombardment, wire cutting, barrages, and time tables, liaison.

(*k*) Action of massed machine guns, including arrangements for indirect fire, barrages, and time tables.

(*l*) Action of tanks.

(*m*) Maps to be carried.

(*n*) Liaison officers.

(*o*) Cooperation with aircraft (contact aeroplanes).

(*p*) Employment of engineers and pioneer units after the assault, and preparations for taking forward R.E. material and stores.

(*q*) Collection and escort of prisoners.

Sketches should accompany these instructions in the case of (*b*), (*c*), (*e*), (*p*), and also for the barrages in (*j*) and (*k*). Sufficient copies should be sent to brigades to allow of one being issued to each unit.

5. As the divisional instructions are received, lower formations will issue such portions as affect the troops under their command.

6. OPERATION ORDERS are a final summary of the salient points in the various instructions and must be kept as brief as possible.

The points which should be dealt with in the divisional operation orders are:

(*a*) General objective of corps, with objectives of divisions on the flanks.

(*b*) Objective of the division.

Objective and frontage of assaulting brigades.

(*d*) Line to be consolidated.

(*e*) Assembly position and preliminary moves of divisional reserves.

(*f*) Artillery barrage and time table.

(*g*) Machine-gun barrage and time table.

(*h*) Action of tanks.

(*i*) Employment of gas and smoke.

(*j*) Employment of R.E. and pioneers.

(*k*) Hours at which contact patrols will fly over our line.

(*l*) Hour by which troops are to be in position.

(*m*) Arrangements for synchronization of watches.

(*n*) Position of divisional report center.

The orders for the move up of assaulting troops into their forming-up places should be issued separately, and should not be included in the orders for the attack.

Zero hour will usually be notified separately as soon as it is known.

7. In issuing orders, particularly for operations against improvised trenches when communication trenches are bad and the progress of runners slow, if possible not less than 24 hours should elapse between the time the order leaves divisional headquarters and the hour fixed for the operation.

Less time than this means that the company and platoon commanders, who actually have to carry out the operation, will not have time to complete their arrangements.

Once orders have been issued, they should not be changed at the last minute; this only results in misunderstandings, and probably means the failure of the operation.

It must, however, be realized that attacks, especially after the first position has been carried, have sometimes to be hurried in order to seize a fleeting opportunity. Units must therefore anticipate their orders, as far as possible, by continually carrying on reconnaissance and preparation.

II. OBJECTIVES.

The points affecting the selection of objectives for each body of Infantry within the division in any one operation[1] are as follows:

---

[1] N. B.—Or "bound." If the first operation is so successful as to admit of the Artillery being at once moved forward, and a fresh bombardment commenced under which the advance can be continued, then a new operation has to be undertaken for which fresh orders must be issued, and which will be separated from the first operation by an appreciable pause.

(*a*) No battalion can be expected to carry out more than one heavy assault in a day.

This does not prevent two successive tasks being allotted to a brigade; the first group of objectives being carried by the battalions in front line and the second group of objectives by battalions in second line.

(*b*) The furthest objective allotted to any troops in the division must be within range of effective Artillery support. This affects corps more than divisions.

(*c*) Each body must be given a limited, clearly defined, and definite objective to capture and consolidate.

The flanks of the objective allotted to each formation should, as far as possible, rest on some conspicuous object, or be easily recognizable by all troops.

A ravine should never be fixed as the boundary between the objectives of two adjacent bodies of troops, if this can be avoided. It is usually defended by enfilade and cross machine-gun fire, and is therefore difficult to capture unless the advance is made simultaneously on both sides of it.

(*d*). The distance of the objective from the jumping-off trench will vary with the class of operation being carried out.

In the original attack against a well-established position, the leading battalions of a brigade should not, as a rule, be given an objective beyond the front-line system, the battalions in brigade reserve being given the next line as an objective, and the reserve brigades being employed to capture still further objectives if the Artillery arrangements permit.

In attacks against improvised lines, where the obstacles to be crossed, i. e., hostile trenches, are less numerous and further apart, and where the ground between the various hostile lines is not so broken up by shell fire, the leading battalions may be given objectives 1,000 yards to 1,200 yards from their jumping-off trenches.

(*e*) The assaulting troops must reach their objective with sufficient remaining energy to use their bayonets and dig when they get there.

If the final objective is too far, if a number of hostile trenches have to be crossed, and if the ground is badly cut up by shell fire, the men are liable to drop behind the barrage, and therefore fail to reach their objective; or, if they reach it, they will not be capable, owing to losses and physical exhaustion, to consolidate their position properly. The commander then runs the risk of the troops not being able to withstand the counter attack, and consequently of losing all he has won.

The wisest policy is to make certain of every piece of ground won and not to ask the troops to do too much.

(f) All troops must move direct on their objective. Complicated maneuvers, such as wheels and forming to a flank, must be avoided when possible, although these may occasionally be necessary when a defensive flank has to be formed.

This emphasizes the necessity for jumping-off trenches to be constructed parallel with the objective, so that the men can move straight to their front.

III. COOPERATION BETWEEN ARTILLERY AND INFANTRY.

1. Success in recent operations has been due, more than to anything else, to the Infantry keeping close up to the Artillery barrage, and entering the enemy's trenches immediately the barrage lifts from these trenches and before the hostile garrison have time to man their defenses.

The greatest attention, therefore, must be devoted to this point during training, and the vital importance of following the barrage closely, even at the risk of a few casualities from short bursts, must be impressed on all ranks.

2. (a) The general principles on which the Artillery prepare for and protect the Infantry during the advance, and the methods which the Infantry must adopt to take full advantage of this preparation and protection must therefore be made known to, and thoroughly understood by, every man taking part in an assault. The principles of preparation and protection will be considered separately.

(b) Artillery, if its fire is to be directed both effectively and quickly, must be furnished with information from all available sources with the least possible delay. Great stress should be laid on this point in the training of Infantry, who must be taught the vital importance, in their own interest, of rapidly transmitting information to the guns that support them.

3. *Preliminary bombardment*—(a) *Object.*—This is the *preparation* of the attack, its object being to demolish the enemy's trenches and works as far as it is desirable to do so, to destroy wire entanglements and other obstacles that would impede the advance of the assaulting troops, to cause casualties and loss of morale among the garrison of the enemy's trenches, to destroy or block communication trenches, to deny to the enemy the ar-

rival of reinforcements, ammunition, and supplies, and to destroy the enemy's artillery.

(b) *Plan.*[1]—The plan for this preliminary bombardment is made out by the G.O.C., R. A., Corps, under the orders of the corps commander, and provides for the employment of all the Artillery resources of the corps, the cooperation of the Artillery of corps on either flank being coordinated by the G.O.C., R.A., Army, under the orders of the Army Commander.

(c) *Destruction of enemy trenches and works.*—Before the Infantry are ordered to attack the ground, maps and aeroplane photographs are thoroughly studied and every point whence the enemy might bring rifle and machine-gun fire to bear upon the ground between the jumping-off trench and the objective is either demolished or noted for subsequent treatment.

The extent to which the enemy's trenches and works should be destroyed has become a matter for serious consideration. If they are entirely demolished, no dugouts or other cover will be left for the use of our Infantry, and this has been found by experience to constitute a grave disadvantage in the case of trenches which have to be held when gained.

This task is principally allotted to howitzers, heavy, medium, and field, and to heavy trench mortars. Guns can, however, be employed with advantage against breastworks, barricades, houses, and other vertical targets.

Photographs showing the progress of the work of demolition are taken daily when conditions are favorable, and issued to all divisional commanders concerned as well as to the corps commander; divisional commanders must satisfy themselves that all danger points in their zones are adequately dealt with, and they should bring to the notice of the corps commander any points which, in their opinion, require more treatment before the Infantry start.

In considering the state of the enemy's defenses as disclosed by photographs, it must be remembered that considerable further effect will be achieved by the bombardment which remains to be carried out between the time that the last photograph is taken and zero hour on the day of attack; and also by the howitzer bombardment which lifts forward from trench to trench from zero hour onwards.

---

[1] N. B.—The general control and direction of the Artillery operations rests with the Army Commander who may direct the G.O.C., R.A. of the Army to issue detailed instructions to Artillery formations.

(*d*) *Wire cutting.*—This is the principal task of the 18-pounders and medium trench mortars, and is carried out in each divisional zone by the Field Artillery allotted to that zone, any assistance required from neighboring Field Artillery units being arranged by the G.O.C., R. A., Corps. Wire which can not be cut by 18-pounders or trench mortars may be satisfactorily attacked by field or medium howitzers using nondelay fuzes.

Wire cutting demands the closest cooperation between the Artillery and Infantry. Commanders of assaulting battalions should visit the O.P.'s of the batteries cutting the wire on their front to watch the progress of the work and should inform the battery commanders when they consider that the wire has been properly cut. In addition, patrols should be sent out nightly during wire cutting to examine and report on the progress made during the day.

Once gaps have been made, it is the duty of divisional commanders to employ all means at their disposal to keep these gaps open during the hours of darkness throughout the period of the preparatory bombardment. These means include the use of rifle and machine-gun fire, rifle grenades, etc. Much artillery ammunition can thus be saved and so can be used for strengthening the fire on communication trenches and other approaches.

(*e*) *Inflicting casualties on the enemy, etc.*—The Artillery will also aim at causing the enemy loss, other than that involved by destructive fire against defenses, by harassing working and ration parties, infilading communication trenches, roads, tracks, and other approaches, and shelling railway stations, dumps, and rest billets. With these objects, fire is delivered at irregular intervals by day and more particularly by night.

Infantry can cooperate with the Artillery against many of these objectives by means of direct and indirect machine-gun fire.

(*f*) *Counter battery work.*—Endeavor is made to destroy as many hostile batteries as possible. This work of destruction is essentially the task of medium and heavy howitzers, and is regarded in principle as an unceasing procedure and not one that is only carried out during a preliminary bombardment or actual attack. Beyond this, all known hostile batteries are either carefully registered or recorded. so that they may be subjected to a violent neutralization fire at the moment of assault, at which time also all known enemy observation stations will be engaged.

(*g*) *Duration of the bombardment.*—Whether the attack is made from our original trenches or after the enemy's main position has been captured is a question directly affecting the duration of the bombardment and the amount of artillery allotted to each of the above tasks.

In the first case, the enemy's trench system will be strong and complicated and a large amount of destruction will be required, whereas the number of enemy guns will probably be comparatively small and counter battery work will consequently not be heavy; the preliminary bombardment may last several days.

In the second case, the enemy's trench system will be weaker, less destruction will be required, but he will probably have concentrated more guns, thus necessitating heavier counter battery work; the bombardment in this case may be only a matter of a few hours.

4. *Protection during the attack.*—This is effected by counter battery work, the howitzer bombardment and by the barrage.

(*a*) *Counter battery work.*—At the moment of assault, all known hostile batteries which might interfere with the advance are subjected to an intense bombardment by long-range guns and howitzers, with the object of destroying the actual guns or of preventing the enemy detachments from serving their guns. This latter procedure is known as neutralizing fire.

(*b*) *Howitzer bombardment.*—At the moment of assault, howitzers, other than those employed on counter battery work, commence an intense bombardment of the enemy's trenches and works, lifting off each line of trenches as soon as the advance of the Infantry brings the latter near the danger zone of our own shells. The time of each lift is worked out accordingly and included in a program which is issued to all concerned.

This bombardment works forward well beyond the objective and then remains stationary on trenches, hollow roads, woods, villages, etc., where the enemy might assemble for a counter attack.

The effect of this bombardment can be increased if indirect machine-gun fire is brought to bear simultaneously on the areas which are being bombarded, with a view to dealing with any of the enemy who attempt to escape the bombardment by leaving their trenches, etc. (See Sec. XVI, par. 2.)

(*c*) The whole of the Artillery arrangements for (*a*) and (*b*) will be worked out, coordinated, and controlled by the G.O.C., R.A., Corps, under the orders of the corps commander.

(d) *The Field Artillery barrage.*—Immediately the advance begins the 18-pounders commence an intense bombardment, with the object of forcing the enemy to take cover and thereby prevent him manning his defenses before the Infantry reach the trench.[1]

At the moment laid down in the time table of Artillery fire, the barrage lifts clear of the trench, and the Infantry then rush in and capture it; all ranks of the Infantry must therefore be taught that success depends on their getting within 50 yards or so (depending on the range) of the barrage before it lifts, in order that the time which elapses between the barrage lifting and the Infantry entering the trench may be less than that required by the enemy to man their parapets. This latter is a matter of a few seconds. It must be remembered that the barrage, following the trace of the trench, will rarely be in a straight line, and the Infantry must be trained to advance accordingly.

The barrage does not necessarily lift direct from one trench to another, but may creep slowly forward, sweeping all the ground between them in order to deal with any machine guns or riflemen pushed out into shell holes in front of or behind the trenches. This creeping barrage will dwell for a certain time on the trench to be assaulted. The Infantry must be trained to follow close behind the barrage from the instant it commences and, then taking advantage of this " dwell," to work up as close as possible to the objective, ready to rush it at the moment that the barrage lifts.

If the barrage is well placed, is sufficiently dense, and extends well beyond the flanks of the actual attack, Infantry can kneel down under the barrage and await the appointed moment of assault.

5. *Pace of the barrage.*—(a) The secret of a successful assault rests upon the assumption that the Infantry conform their movements exactly to the timing of the barrage. The importance of this timing, therefore, can not be overestimated.

If the lifts are too quick, the pace will be too fast, and the Infantry will fail to keep up with the barrage. Once this happens the whole advantage of the barrage will be lost, as the

---

[1] NOTE.—It is to be understood that this indicates the procedure which has recently been most successful. Artillery methods must, however, constantly be reviewed, and, if necessary, modified to suit changing tactical conditions.

enemy will have time to man his parapet before the Infantry reaches it. The advance will then be brought to a standstill under close-range enemy-rifle and machine-gun fire, while the barrage moves further and further away in accordance with the time-table.

If there is too long a pause between each lift, the pace will be too slow, and the rear waves will push on too fast and become mixed up with the leading waves, thereby forming a thicker line and increasing casualties, besides losing the driving power which a series of waves gives to the attack.

(*b*) It is impossible to lay down any definite ruling as to the best pace; it must be regulated entirely by local conditions.

The state of the weather, the extent to which the ground is cut up by shell fire, the length of the advance, the number of enemy trenches to be crossed, all affect the pace at which the Infantry, and consequently the barrage, can move. In actual practice the pace has varied from 75 yards a minute, when conditions were very favorable, to 15 yards a minute when they were very unfavorable.

(*c*) A uniform pace throughout the advance is unsound; at the commencement the pace of the barrage should be quicker, gradually slowing down toward the finish as the men become exhausted, in order to give them time to get close up to the barrage and to pull themselves together for the final rush.

In the case of a long advance it is advisable to keep the barrage on the objective for a double period, in order to make quite certain that the men are closed up and ready to rush the trench.

Above all, it is essential that in the attack of a more or less intact system of defense the Infantry should cross " No Man's Land " as quickly as possible. To achieve this it is of vital importance that the Infantry should start off at zero time with absolute punctuality, for any delay at this moment may be disastrous.

6. *Time-tables.*—The timing of the barrage is fixed, as part of the corps Artillery plan, by the corps commander after consultation with divisional commanders, particular attention being paid to the points of junction between divisions to insure that the barrages on each divisional front overlap properly.

The timings worked out are then embodied in a program or time-table and issued to all concerned.

The duration of the barrage depends on the number of objectives to be gained.

Where there is only one objective the barrage, after lifting off the objective, will continue to creep forward till it reaches a line about 300 yards beyond the objective. This distance is necessary to give room for outposts to be pushed out to cover the consolidation.

The barrage then becomes stationary and gradually dies down, ceasing altogether as soon as the Infantry report that they have secured the objective.

When there is another objective there will be a certain pause, previously arranged and laid down, to enable the troops detailed for the assault of the next objective to get into position; the barrage will then commence moving forward again in accordance with the time-table.

7. *Control of the barrage.*—(*a*) The control of the barrage remains in the hands of the corps commander throughout the assault, but in order that divisional commanders may be able to deal promptly with any situation which may arise on their front they will be given a call on a certain number of batteries (18-pounders, 4.5-inch, and 6-inch howitzers) from the commencement of the assault.

All batteries thus detailed will have tasks allotted to them in accordance with corps orders, and will carry them out unless and until their assistance is demanded by the divisional commander concerned.

The divisional commander will demand the assistance of these batteries through the commander of all the Field Artillery supporting his division. The latter officer will have his headquarters at divisional headquarters, if possible, and will be in direct communication with all the Field Artillery groups under him and also with the G.O.C., R.A., corps.

(*b*) To enable commanders of assaulting brigades to take immediate action in any situation which may arise the divisional commander may delegate to the brigadiers concerned the power to call direct on some of the batteries placed at his disposal.

The brigadier will call on these batteries through the commander of the Field Artillery directly supporting his brigade. This latter officer will, whenever possible, establish his headquarters in the immediate vicinity of the Infantry brigade headquarters, but where this is not possible he will maintain the closest touch with the Infantry brigadier by means of a senior Artillery liaison officer.

The governing factor as to which of these two methods should be followed is to a great extent a question of communications. Unforeseen situations will always arise necessitating the passage of orders and information between a divisional C.R.A. and his group commanders. If the headquarters of an Infantry brigade is so placed that communication between an Artillery group commander at or near those headquarters and his divisional C.R.A. has a reasonable prospect of remaining continuously open, such is the best solution. If not, then the Artillery group commander is better represented by a responsible liaison officer.

(c) Except when minor operations by single battalions are being carried out, it will usually be unnecessary to give O.'s.C. assaulting battalions the power to call on batteries, and consequently these officers will not require Artillery liaison officers.

8. *Signals from Infantry to Artillery.*—(a) For the first hour or so after the assault, until communications can be well established, touch between the Infantry and their supporting Artillery will generally be restricted by force of circumstances to calls for barrage fire by means of light signal rockets. Infantry commanders must therefore insure that their leading troops are equipped with an ample supply of these rockets before the assault.

(b) Colored flags, carried by one or two men in each platoon, can be used to indicate to the Artillery the line gained by the leading Infantry.

These flags must not be stuck in the ground and will mean nothing unless they are waved; the poles should be short and blunted at the end.

A combination of black and yellow on a flag about 18 inches square is the easiest to observe.

(c) The position of the leading Infantry has been successfully indicated to aeroplane observers (and so transmitted to the Artillery) by the lighting of flares at certain prearranged times or at an agreed signal from the aeroplane.

9. (a) In all practice assaults during training the time table for the barrage lifts must be worked out.

The creeping barrage can be represented by smoke screens formed by smoke bombs, by canvas screens raised and lowered as required, or, in the case of large units, by mounted men, carrying colored flags, under an Artillery officer.

The Infantry must be trained to realize that their own probable rate of advance is the governing factor affecting that of the barrage, and that, the pace of the barrage having been decided, it is essential that they should start with precise punctuality and advance close up under the barrage, as already explained.

(*b*) When ammunition is available, it has been found useful to arrange for demonstrations of an actual creeping barrage, when the troops are in the line.

The battery or batteries covering a battalion front can put on a barrage with three or four lifts; the barrage should commence in "No Man's Land" and lift on to the enemy's front, support, and reserve lines in succession.

As many men of the battalion as possible should watch this barrage.

Every battalion in the division should be given one such demonstration while in the trenches.

The value obtained from these demonstrations is clearly shown when the training ground is reached.

IV. Formations and Frontages.

1. (*a*) These two are interdependent, the guiding principle being that each unit must have sufficient driving power in itself to carry it through to its objective and to maintain itself when it gets there; therefore it must be formed in depth.

(*b*) Where a number of trenches have to be carried before the objective is reached, considerable depth will be required to give the necessary driving power; therefore the frontage allotted to the unit must be reduced. This will be the case in the original attack. In later attacks the objective may be only one or two lines of trenches; less depth will then be required to give the necessary driving power, and therefore increased frontages can be allotted.

(*c*) Experience has shown that a front of 300 to 350 yards is sufficient for a battalion with an average assaulting strength of 800 (600 to 700 yards for a brigade with two battalions in front line) in the original assault against a well-established position; this may have to be reduced to 250, or even 200 yards, if a battalion has to carry a particularly strong fortified point, such as a village or wood.

(*d*) In later stages of the attack, where the enemy position is not so well organized, a battalion may be given a frontage of 600 yards (1,200 yards for a brigade with two battalions in front line).

2. To produce the necessary driving power the battalion must be organized in depth in a series of waves.

(*a*) The first two or three waves will move in line extended to three or four or even five paces. These waves are more likely to meet with machine-gun fire, and therefore should present as unfavorable a target as possible.

The rear waves will move either in a line or in section columns in single file. In the original assault, where enemy machine guns are likely to be more trouble than the enemy barrage, lines will probably be most suitable. In later stages, when the enemy barrage is the dominating factor, the waves should preferably move in small handy columns, which can pick their way through a barrage with fewer casualties than an extended line, and which are more readily controlled and easier to maneuver.

(*b*) The distance between waves requires to be carefully worked out. In the original assault, when the enemy's barrage is not likely to be intense, the waves may be 75 to 100 yards apart, in order to minimize the casualties from machine-gun fire. In later stages as many waves as possible must be started before the hostile barrage comes down, and it will then be necessary for the waves to follow each other at 50 yards distance or even less.

3. The functions and composition of the various waves require some consideration.

(*a*) The leading waves are the fighting men; their primary job is to get to the objective as quickly as possible and bayonet or capture the garrison. Men lightly equipped, armed with the rifle and bayonet and a few bombs, are required for this work.

Behind them come consolidation parties, carrying parties, and the reserve.

(*b*) The position of bombers, Lewis gunners, scouts, snipers, etc., in the various waves, and their duties are dealt with under their respective headings.

4. (*a*) In addition to the various parties mentioned in paragraph 3, there is the *all*-important " *cleaning* " or " *mopping-up* " *party*.

The greatest care and attention must be paid to their training and organization, and every man must know exactly what he has to do.

(*b*) As a rule the leading waves do their own mopping up, when the objective has been reached; but in reaching it they have to pass over a number of trenches, whose garrisons are temporarily hiding in dugouts to escape our barrage; these garrisons reappear very quickly, and must be promptly dealt with ⌐ moppers up.

(c) Where the objective is limited to a single trench, the assaulting companies can do their own mopping up. In other cases the moppers up should be drawn from another company in the battalion or possibly from another battalion in the brigade. The party detailed for each trench must be under a selected officer of their own unit.

Moppers up should always wear a distinguishing mark. (See Sec. XXXII.)

(d) When moppers up belong to the assaulting unit, there is a danger that the moppers up, in the excitement of the attack, will continue to press forward with their comrades and fail to carry out their task, thus exposing the leading troops to the danger of being shot in the back.

When the moppers up are drawn from a separate unit, this danger is not so likely to occur.

(e) The strength of the mopping-up parties depends on the number of trenches to be cleaned up; normally 25 per cent of the assaulting column (i. e., one company for a battalion) will be sufficient; but when assaulting strongly fortified villages, or woods, 50 per cent, or even 100 per cent, will be required.

(f) The mopping-up parties should follow immediately behind the leading wave, so that they may lose no time in getting to work. Where more than two separate parties are required, the parties detailed for the third and subsequent trenches should move immediately behind the second wave, as by the time the third trench is reached, the second wave will have begun to close up on and absorb the leading wave.

(g) On arrival in their allotted trench, moppers up must at once dispose of any occupants who have emerged from their dugouts, at the same time picketing the dugout entrances to prevent any more coming out. As soon as the trench has been cleared, parties must be despatched to clear the communication trenches forward as far as the next line of trench, while the remainder clean out the dugouts already picketed.

P. grenades are most effective for the latter work, as Mills grenades have little effect on really deep, well-organized dugouts; the latter are, however, required for clearing the trenches, in addition to the rifle and bayonet.

As soon as every place has been cleared, the prisoners are collected and sent off under a small escort, while the rest of the party proceeds to consolidate and garrison the captured trench.

5. The ultimate unit in the assault is the PLATOON. The platoon must be organized and trained as a self-contained unit

capable of producing the required proportions of riflemen, rifle bombers, bombers, carriers, and runners trained to work in combination. One or two Lewis guns may also be added on occasion. On the resourcefulness and self-sufficiency of the platoon in dealing scientifically with every obstacle which it may meet, on its internal organization into small parties trained to their particular tasks under their own leaders, and on the skill of the platoon leader and the hold which he has over his command, the success of the assault will largely depend.

V. THE ASSAULT.

1. When conditions are favorable, i. e., when there is plenty of dugout accommodation available, assaulting troops should take over their jumping-off trenches in sufficient time to give them 12 hours of daylight in the trenches before the assault. This gives all ranks time to make themselves thoroughly acquainted with the ground over which they have to advance, and to make any final arrangements required; it also enables the men to get some rest before the assault, which is impossible when they have to spend the night previous to the assault in a relief.

2. Where trenches are poor and dugouts few the assaulting troops should be kept out of the trenches as long as possible to avoid exposing them to hostile shelling.

3. Arrangements must be made to give all ranks a hot meal and a rum ration before the assault.

4. It is not possible to lay down a definite signal for the Infantry to leave their trenches and to commence the assault for use on all occasions.

In the original attack where the enemy's barrage is not likely to be heavy, zero may be fixed for the moment at which our barrage lifts from the enemy front trench, the Infantry timing their advance so as to be close under our barrage before it lifts.

In the later stages, when the enemy, being on the alert, may be expected to put down a heavy barrage very quickly, it is essential that the Infantry should all start together. Zero, then, must be the moment at which our barrage commences, and this commencement will be the signal for the Infantry to leave their trenches.

5. The leading wave must go straight through to its objective, following the barrage as close as possible. Intervening hostile

trenches must be crossed as quickly as possible, the line reformed on the far side, and the advance resumed.

6. All movement must be over the top of the ground.

The pace throughout should be a steady walk, except for the last 30 or 40 yards before reaching each trench, when the line should break into a steady double, finishing up the last 10 yards with a rush.

7. If the line is checked by the barrage not moving fast enough, the men must get as close to it as possible and kneel down; they must not be allowed to lie down, as it is difficult to get them started again.

8. Where men have been previously trained, good results can be obtained, especially in wooded country, if the men of the leading wave fire from the hip as they advance. This fire acts as covering fire and helps the barrage to keep the enemy's heads down.

If firing is permitted, the men must *not halt to fire.*

9. Officers and N.C.O.'s must advance strictly in line with their men.

10. The necessity for careful synchronization of watches is apparent; a delay of 30 seconds in starting by one company may mean its failure to get in, and may possibly lead to the dislocation or failure of the whole attack.

11. Every precaution must be taken to prevent the enemy realizing that the assault is about to take place. Bayonets must not be allowed to show over the parapet or in communication trenches; there must be no increase in the rate of artillery fire, no sudden and unusual movement in the trenches. The enemy must be kept in the dark until the barrage commences; otherwise he will put down his own barrage and possibly prevent our attack from leaving our own trenches.

12. It is advisable, especially in cases where our front jumping-off trench is not absolutely square with the direction of the advance, to mark out the forming-up line, in front of our trenches, with broad white tape pegged down with iron staples.

This tape can be put out the night previous to the assault by the battalion scouts, who should be provided with compasses to insure that the tape is laid out on the correct alignment; it should be put out also in front of those trenches behind the front line, from which the rear waves will start.

When the assault is made during the hours of darkness, the forming-up line for each wave must be taped out.

13. The hour at which the assault is to be delivered requires consideration. In large operations, where more than one division is concerned, the hour is settled by the corps or army.

Where the divisional commander has to fix the hour himself, the following points have to be considered:

(*a*) A daylight attack is the best for the following reasons:

(1) Final preparations can be completed by daylight.

(2) The men are fresher and have more vitality.

(3) Cooperation with artillery is easier.

The attack should take place as late as possible, provided that sufficient daylight is allowed for all objectives to be carried, and consolidation to be well under way before darkness sets in.

(*b*) A dawn attack may have to be made—

(1) When the trenches are poor and when the assaulting troops can not be assembled in them without being seen by the enemy.

(2) When tanks are cooperating, as they must be got into position under cover of darkness.

(3) As a sequel to a night advance, when " No Man's Land " is wide, and it has not been possible to push our jumping-off trenches any nearer the enemy.

(*c*) Night attacks should be avoided if possible.

(1) Night advances and night attacks demand complete possession of " No Man's Land " by our patrols, especially in the case of the former.

The state of the weather and the time of the year must also be taken into account.

(2) Before a night attack, troops should be in position at least six hours before dark to give time for reconnaissance.

Similarly, before a night alvance they should be in the trenches, from which the advance will be made, at least six hours before dark.

VI. Action of Reserves.

1. It is a golden rule that all commanders, down to and including company commanders, must keep some portion of their command (usually about 25 per cent) in hand as a reserve.

2. This does not mean that the reserves are to be kept back and jealously guarded until the time for their action has arisen; if this is done, they will invariably arrive too late.

On the other hand, reserves should not be pushed forward in rear of the asaulting columns without a definite task; otherwise they get lost and soon cease to be reserves at all.

3. From the moment the assault starts there must be a steady flow of troops forward throughout the division; but those in rear must not be allowed to wander on aimlessly and must be checked at certain prearranged lines where fresh orders can be sent.

4. The art of making the utmost use of reserves depends on the amount of forethought which has been devoted to their probable action; commanders of every grade must think out, as far as possible, every situation which may arise and have plans ready to deal with each one. These plans must be communicated to the officers under them beforehand.

5. The company commander requires a reserve for three purposes:

(*a*) To assist his own company to get forward by working quickly around the flanks of any point which may be holding up his leading lines.

(*b*) To protect his flanks in the event of the companies on his right or left being hung up.

This protection must be obtained by pushing in his reserve on the exposed flank and acting vigorously on the offensive. Thus he will not only protect himself but also make it easier for the unit which is temporarily hung up to get forward.

(*c*) If his attack succeeds in reaching its objective, he still requires a body of troops, well in hand, to exploit his success and gain ground to the front. This point is dealt with later.

He must, therefore, move forward behind his company with his reserve well in hand, ready to throw it into the fight wherever it is required.

6. The battalion commander requires a reserve for the same purposes as the company commander, and also for the purpose of throwing back, or extending, a flank in the event of the battalion on his right or left failing to get forward.

The handling of this reserve requires some consideration. It must start with the assaulting column and get across " No Man's Land " as soon as possible, but it must not be allowed to push on too far, otherwise there is a risk of it becoming mixed up in the fight and getting out of hand, and consequently not being available when required. It seems preferable, therefore, to check its advance in the vicinity of the enemy front-line trench

The battalion commander will then know where to lay his hands on it when he wants it.

The battalion commander must think out beforehand the most probable situations which may arise and explain these, together with his proposed plan for dealing with each situation, to the commander of the reserve, in order that, when the time arrives for action, the latter officer will know his C.O.'s ideas, and no time will be lost in lengthy explanations.

7. (a) The handling of his reserve by the brigade commander requires somewhat different treatment to those of the battalion and company commander; he must keep a tighter hold on it, as, in addition to the possible tasks already outlined for the reserves of the lower formations, it is probable that there will be a second objective, which his reserve will have to take as soon as the leading battalions have taken the first objective.

(b) If the reserve follows on automatically behind the assaulting battalions, there is a risk of it becoming mixed up in the failure of one of the leading battalions and becoming dispersed, with the result that the brigade commander will lose control of it and will be unable to throw it in where it could effect the most good—i. e., on the flank of the unit which had failed.

(c) Its advance, therefore, should be checked before it reaches our front-line trench, and it should halt, awaiting further orders, in a handy formation, capable of being moved in any direction.

The hostile barrage is usually put down on our front and support-line trenches; therefore the reserve should be halted just clear of this area to avoid being broken up unnecessarily by shell fire.

(d) In any case it will not be possible to get this reserve across " No Man's Land " before the barrage comes down, and therefore it is preferable to keep it clear of the barrage as orders can then reach it quicker, and it can be maneuvered more easily.

(e) Where the Artillery preparations permit of the assault on the second objective following immediately on that of the first, the brigade commander, as soon as he hears that the assault of his leading battalions is progressing satisfactorily, although he may not yet have information that they have reached their objective, should send off the reserve to capture its objective.

(f) The reserve should then move off at once, in Artillery formation, through the barrage, and continue in that formation as long as possible, passing straight through the leading battalions. Even if the leading battalions are still held up short of their objective, the appearance of a fresh body of troops on the field will have a great moral effect and will probably enable the leading battalions to push in.

(*g*) The position of the commander of this reserve at the outset requires consideration. It will probably be found that the best place will be at the headquarters of one of the assaulting battalions. Here he will be in touch with his brigadier and will also get the information as to the progress of the attack quicker than if he were at brigade headquarters, and thus will be able to anticipate his orders.

8. (*a*) The possible tasks for the divisional reserve are more varied. They may be required for any of the following purposes:

> (1) The capture of a further objective, the reserve passing through the troops, who have already reached their objectives.
>
> (2) To relieve the assaulting brigades, which may have captured their objective but which may be, owing to losses, too weak to hold the captured line against counter-attacks.
>
> (3) To relieve troops who have failed with a view to making another attack after Artillery preparation.
>
> (4) To form a defensive flank in case of failure by divisions on the flanks.

(*b*) As regards (1) this is the task which will be uppermost in the divisional commander's mind, and for which he will make all preliminary arrangements.

(*c*) These arrangements will include moving the reserve forward at zero to a prearranged position, as near our original front line as possible, without exposing it unnecessarily to shell fire and assembling the reserve there in such a formation as will enable it to be moved quickly and easily in any direction and will give the men as much rest as possible.

(*d*) The commander of the reserve should establish his report center at, or in close proximity to, the headquarters of one of the leading brigades and should assemble his battalion commanders at this point so that he can keep in touch with them.

(*e*) He himself, with one staff officer, should remain with the divisional commander. This enables him to watch the general situation develop, to obtain all the information available, and to discuss the probable tasks with the divisional commander. Thus, when the time arrives for action, he is fully aware of the situation, and the divisional commander has not to waste time in explaining it to him, but will give him brief, definite orders to carry on in accordance with the plan previously arranged.

(*f*) The arrangements required for (1) will hold good equally for (2), (3), and (4), the only difference in (3) and (4) being that action will be required earlier than in the other two cases.

9. The reserves of companies and battalions must, of course, start moving over the top of the ground with the rest of the assaulting troops.

The reserves of brigades and of the division can be moved up to their positions of readiness, either above ground or through trenches, in accordance with the amount of cover available.

Once they are ordered to move forward for a definite task all movement must be above ground.

10. Divisional and brigade commanders must not be afraid to use their reserves. If things are going well nothing is gained by holding back reserves to meet situations which may not arise. Once the enemy's front line has been captured his state of confusion and demoralization must be increased by continual pressure by fresh troops. No opportunity must be lost of gaining ground before the enemy has time to recover and reorganize.

The man on the spot is the best man to judge when the situation is favorable for pushing on, and higher commanders in rear must be prepared to support the man on the spot to the fullest extent by adjusting the movements of the Artillery barrage and bombardment and by continually pushing forward reserves.

The use of his reserves by the battalion commander to gain ground is more limited, and is considered in detail in Section VIII.

11. The actual task of passing one body of troops through another during an attack is not a difficult operation, as far as the troops themselves are concerned.

Special care, however, is needed in arranging the signal communications.

The easiest way is for the commander of the troops passing through to establish his report center at an existing headquarters of the troops already engaged, where he can receive orders and messages.

Meanwhile reconnáissance must be made for another head-quarters further forward and a wire got out to it.

12. The question of holding the original front line, in case of the failure of the first attack, is one which concerns brigade commanders in the front line.

As has already been mentioned, our front line is a place to be avoided, once the attack has been launched, owing to the hostile barrage.

Therefore the fewer troops detailed to hold it the better.

The cheapest and most effective means of doing this is to detail a section of the machine-gun company; these guns will be sufficient to stop any immediate counterattack by the enemy, and being only a small party will not find it difficult to obtain shelter from the enemy's barrage.

13. The action to be taken by commanders in case the assault fails is closely connected with the handling of the reserves, as has already been pointed out.

The assault may fail either partially or entirely.

14. In the case of a partial failure, the situation can be met by the commanders of units on the flanks which have succeeded, pushing in their reserves immediately to act vigorously against the flanks and rear of the portion of the line which is still holding out; if this is insufficient, further reserves must be thrown in on the same principles, the principles being to avoid frontal assaults and to isolate that portion still holding out and thus enable the general advance to be resumed.

Meanwhile the isolated portion can be dealt with by bombers and Stokes mortars working in from the flanks, assisted where possible by field howitzers; this, however, will take some little time to prepare.

15. (a) In the case of a total failure, where pressure from the flanks has failed to improve the situation, it is a waste of men to put in fresh troops hurriedly to make another assault without any further Artillery preparation, or to attempt a second attack with troops who have already failed. Where an attack has failed after the most careful preparations have been made, it is not reasonable to expect that a second attack launched without any further preparation is likely to succeed.

(b) It is, therefore, cheaper in men and quicker in the long run to adopt more deliberate methods.

The Artillery bombardment must be recommenced as quickly as possible. The troops who have failed must be relieved as soon as possible and sent back out of the shelled area to reorganize and refit.

All other preparations must be made as for the first assault. It is unlikely, therefore, that the second assault can be delivered before at least 48 hours, and probably more, have elapsed.

16. Plenty of practice in dealing with such situations must be given during training.

Umpires can create them by checking the advance of one portion of the line while the rest is allowed to go on. Only in this way can officers develop that initiative and resource which is so necessary in the actual assault to deal with any situation.

VII. CONSOLIDATION.

1. Provided the Artillery preparation has been thorough and complete, and the Infantry have been trained to advance close behind the barrage, the assault will seldom fail; but there remains the task of holding on to what they have gained and of beating off possible counterattacks.

This can only be done successfully when the position has been well consolidated.

2. *Consolidation.*—Consolidation varies in proportion to the care given to the previous preparation and to the amount of attention which has been devoted to it during training; therefore, in all practice assaults consolidation must be carried out, the trenches being actually dug and not merely scratched. The digging must be carried out on a proper system; the absence of proper traverses in trenches consolidated by British troops is still very noticeable.

3. *Counterattacks.*—The counterattacks which troops must be prepared to meet after capturing a position are of two kinds:

(a) An immediate counterattack delivered within from five minutes to half an hour by local supports and reserves launched without any Artillery preparation.

(b) A deliberate counterattack, generally on a fairly large scale, delivered by fresh troops and preceded by Artillery preparation and an intense bombardment. This attack is unlikely to be delivered within the first six hours at least, as time is required for its preparation.

Troops should have no difficulty in repulsing the first, which will usually be spasmodic and flurried if covering parties have been put out; bomb stops are made to block all covered approaches, and the men use their rifles.

Protection against the second depends principally on the progress made in our consolidation and in opening up communications with the rear. Even if no counterattack takes place, heavy hostile shelling is certain sooner or later, so that the ultimate safety of all ranks depends largely upon the intensity with which they dig.

4. *Outpost line.*—(*a*) On reaching the objective the provision of a covering force or outpost line to cover the consolidation is the first consideration.

This outpost line must be established immediately the objective is reached, it must be pushed out 100 to 200 yards beyond the line to be consolidated, and as close as possible to the final barrage line. The commander of each assaulting company is responsible for thus protecting his own front.

(*b*) The outpost line is formed by a line of small self-contained posts, each consisting of an N.C.O., about 6 riflemen, and a Lewis gun. These posts are required about every 150 to 200 yards along the front and should establish themselves in some convenient shell hole, the shell hole being converted as rapidly as possible into a short length of fire trench.

(*c*) Communication trenches running toward the enemy from the captured line must be double blocked, and bombers, both hand and rifle, posted at the block, together with a Stokes mortar as soon as it can be got up. (See Sec. XX, par. 4.)

Snipers posted where they can enfilade these communication trenches can do good service. (See Sec. XVIII.)

(*d*) This outpost line is sufficient to deal with the immediate counterattacks.

It will also help considerably to break up the more deliberate attacks; owing to its distance in front of the main line it will probably not be discovered, and therefore will escape most of the hostile shelling; it will consequently come as a surprise to the advancing hostile infantry.

5. *Main line.*—Meanwhile the consolidation of the main line must be pushed on as fast as possible.

The first step is to convert the captured trench into a fire trench facing the enemy by forming a fire step and building up the parados into a parapet.

Where the captured trench is very much knocked about by our bombardment, and, especially in the later stages, where the enemy trenches are fewer, and therefore better known to their own artillery, it is usually advisable, both on the score of time and of immunity from shelling, to consolidate an entirely new trench 40 to 50 yards in advance of the captured line. This can be done quickly by joining up shell holes, the first essential being to get a continuous trench from which men can use their rifles.

6. As soon as this has been done parties should be detailed—

(a) To open up the entrances of and clear any existing dug-outs; traverses will probably have to be built to protect the entrances from hostile shell fire.

(b) To dig communication trenches forward to the posts in the outpost line.

(c) To commence opening up communication trenches to the rear, either by clearing out existing ones or digging fresh ones.

(d) To dig deep, narrow slits, running off the fire trench, to give the garrison some protection against hostile shelling.

(e) To collect S.A.A., grenades, flares, Very's lights, tools, rations, water, etc., and form dumps at suitable places.

7. *Reorganization.*—When this consolidation is nearing completion the next step is the thinning of the line. This is necessary for two reasons:

(a) It is unsound to have too many men in the captured trench; they can not all find cover from the hostile shelling, and therefore will suffer more or less heavy casualties.

(b) The battalion commander must reorganize his unit in depth in order to provide supports and reserves for counter-attacks.

Also, he may be required to send troops forward in support of other troops who have passed through his line to capture a further objective.

This point requires the personal attention of the commanding officer, who must try to get his unit reorganized as early as possible into a fighting unit.

8. *Strong points.*—(a) In addition to the consolidation of the captured line the construction of strong points of resistance to give additional depth to the defense must be taken in hand.

These will be constructed by the field companies working under the C.R.E. (See Sec. IX, par. 5 (a).)

(b) They will consist of small posts, designed for a garrison of about 20 rifles and 1 or 2 machine guns, and located 200 to 300 yards in rear of the consolidated line.

(c) The siting of these works will largely depend on the existence of dugouts or of good, natural cover, such as sunken roads, banks, quarries, etc. It must be remembered, however, that the enemy will know the naturally strong points of his late position and is sure to bombard them heavily.

(*d*) The type of work selected must be simple, quick to make, and designed so that it can be further strengthened and improved with time.

A type which has been found very useful is the " crucifix " type:

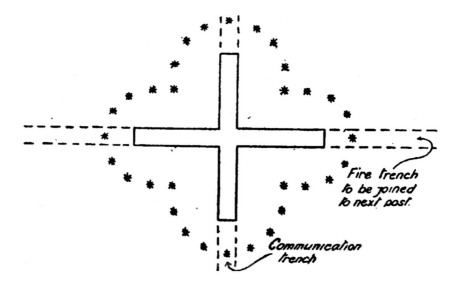

The post is made with the necessary traverses and of irregular shape, according to the configuration of the ground.

It attracts less attention from the enemy's artillery than circular or rectangular posts, while providing sufficient all-round fire, and a greater number of rifles to the front than can be obtained from a circular or rectangular post for the same-sized garrison.

(*e*) Garrisons for these posts must be detailed beforehand and they must be ready to take them over as soon as the R.E. report them ready for occupation.

9. *Communication trenches.*—Further in rear again will be parties of pioneers and infantry, working under the C.R.E., opening up new communication trenches or clearing out old ones from our jumping-off trench across " No Man's Land," and forward to the captured line, where they will join up with those which the troops in the captured line have commenced to dig toward the rear.

10. Consolidation carried out on the lines indicated above will in a very few hours provide the nucleus of a defensive sys-

tem, consisting of a firing line (the outpost line), a support line (the consolidated trench), with a line of strong points further in rear.

11. The use of wire, dugout frames, and revetting material needs consideration:

(a) As regards wire, the value of even a single strand in front of the consolidated line in holding up a counter attack requires no explanation; on the other hand, wire and pickets are bulky and require a large carrying party; also its presence assists the enemy in locating the exact trenches which we are holding. The erection of wire in front of the captured line during the early stages of consolidation depends, primarily, on whether men are available for the necessary carrying parties.

In any case the strong points must be wired all around simultaneously with their construction, even if the wiring of the front line has to wait till a later period. It is usually best to detail a special wiring party, the men carrying up their own materials.

(b) It is most important to provide some sort of bombproof cover in the captured trench as soon as possible; on the other hand the transport of the necessary materials requires a large number of men.

This, again, therefore depends on the number of men available, and will usually have to wait.

Even if it is impossible to get up the timber framing required for deep-mined dugouts, it will often be possible to get up the semicircular corrugated iron sections used for constructing the small two-men dog-kennel shelters under the front parapet.

(c) The same remarks apply to revetting materials, of which sandbags only can be got up at the outset; the bulk of the sandbags can be brought up by the assaulting troops themselves, each man carrying two or three.

12. The further stages of the consolidation, i. e., work which must be carried out after the first five or six hours subsequent to the assault, are as follows:

(a) Intermediate posts must be interpolated between the posts in the outpost line and linked up to the main line behind with communication trenches.

Each post must then be extended to the flanks to join up with the posts on either side and thus form a continuous line.

This line then becomes the starting point for the next assault.

The various steps in this operation are shown in the sketch following:

28

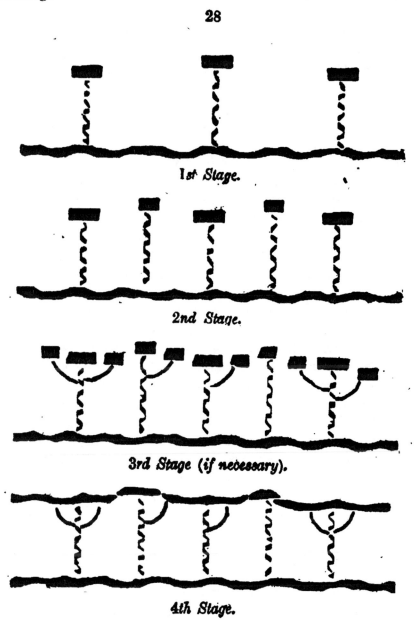

1st Stage.

2nd Stage.

3rd Stage (if necessary).

4th Stage.

(b) The main line must be improved, wired, and provided with bombproof shelter.

(c) The communication trenches leading toward the rear must be widened, improved, and floored with trench gratings.

(d) The strong points must be strengthened and improved; bombproof cover for garrison, especially machine gunners, extended; and the necessary reserves of S.A.A. grenades, food, water, etc., collected and stored.

(e) The intervals between the strong points must be filled with wire, and, if time permits, the strong points themselves must be linked up by a fire trench.

13. *Consolidation of woods and villages.*—This point requires special consideration.

Where woods or villages are allotted as objectives, experience has shown that it is best to push on 200 to 300 yards beyond the far edge and consolidate a line there.

The reasons for this are as follows:

(a) Immediately the enemy realizes that we have captured a wood or a village, he turns a concentrated artillery fire, chiefly heavy H.E., on to it and keeps the locality, particularly his edge of it, under heavy bombardment for a considerable time.

It is very difficult to reorganize troops under these conditions.

(b) It is difficult for our own Artillery to put a barrage immediately in front of the far edge of a wood or village.

(c) It gives room for the defense to be organized in depth, while keeping the men more or less out of the shelled area.

Provision must, however, be made for strong points further back to enable us to maintain our hold on the wood or village, should the enemy counterattack succeed in breaking through our outer defenses, and to provide us with a jumping-off line from which our counterattack, in its turn, can be launched.

In the case of woods, the line of strong points should run inside the wood some 200 yards back from the edge nearest the enemy.

The same principle applies to villages; but in their case one or more strong points, just clear of the village on our side, to guard the exits and to stop a rush of the enemy past the strong points within the village, are required.

VIII. Exploiting Success.

1. Although a commander's first duty on reaching his objective is to make every effort to secure it against recapture by the enemy, this does not imply that he should adopt a purely defensive attitude.

On the contrary, he must continue his offensive with any troops available after the needs of consolidation have been provided for.

2. The enemy is bound to be in confusion immediately after our successful assault; a few men boldly handled will then

usually be able to seize, at practically no cost, important tactical points beyond the objective.

If immediate advantage of the enemy's state of confusion is not taken, the opportunity will be lost, as he recovers very quickly; tactical points which might have been had for the asking will have to be taken later at considerable expense.

3. This "exploiting of success" should be carried out by means of small patrols working quickly forward beyond our outpost line. Other parties, with Lewis guns, must be held ready to back up these patrols and to secure any ground gained.

The patrols should consist of about six men, moving in arrowhead formation; they must act with great dash and boldness, and their leaders require considerable initiative and resource.

4. Should the patrols find a trench, sunken road, village, wood, etc., unoccupied, they must occupy it and send back information to their unit. The patrol must not return as a whole to report, otherwise the enemy will probably have reoccupied the position before the troops sent to hold it reach there. The addition of a signaler, equipped with a flag or signaling shutter, to each patrol is valuable.

5. The distance beyond the objective to which these patrols should go can not be definitely laid down. While it is undesirable for isolated detachments to push on too far ahead, where they are beyond reach of support and liable to be surrounded and cut off, yet the importance of seizing tactical features when the opportunity offers is so great that commanders are justified in taking some risks.

The decision must be left to the man on the spot; he is more likely to arrive at a correct decision if he knows the intentions of the higher commander as to the subsequent action and the probable movements of the units on his flanks. Brigadiers must, therefore, insure that all officers are given any information available on these points.

6. The moment at which to send these patrols forward requires consideration.

For the first 20 minutes or half an hour after the objective has been reached our barrage will still continue, though its intensity will be growing less every minute.

The patrols, therefore, must work forward to the edge of the barrage and wait till either it ceases or they can seize an opportunity of passing through it as it becomes less intense.

7. In order not to hamper the action of these patrols, arrangements must be made as regards our barr

probably best to decide beforehand approximately the localities for which these patrols should make, and then to arrange that, after a certain hour, the barrage will be extended to include those localities. The patrols will act more boldly if they feel that they are not likely to be cut off by our own barrage.

8. The parties detailed to back up the patrols and confirm their success must move forward by bounds, securing the ground by means of their Lewis guns at each step of the advance.

9. As soon as the new line has been occupied it must be consolidated in the same way as the original objective. An outpost line must be established in front and further parties must be sent up to assist in the consolidation. This line, instead of the original objective, then becomes the battle front.

In favorable circumstances it has been found possible to advance the line 500 yards by this method within an hour of the objective having been reached.

10. Success in this depends, as in every other operation, on the amount of previous training and preparation. Therefore it must always be practiced during training.

IX. Employment of R.E. and Pioneers.

1. The actual employment of the field companies and pioneer battalion of the division will usually rest with the divisional commander. In addition the corps may allot him certain field companies or pioneers from the reserve divisions and tunneling companies or army troops companies if required.

2. To obtain the best results from the R.E. and pioneers, it is essential to allot them definite tasks, as far as possible, as they require time to organize their work and to collect the necessary materials. The divisional commander must, however, retain a proportion in his own hand for use in unforeseen emergencies; if possible, not more than half the R.E. and pioneers available should be employed at the outset.

3. It is more economical and better in every way to employ these technical units directly under the C.R.E.; brigadiers are fully employed during an action in handling their own commands and can not give the time and attention required to handle outside units.

4. The tasks, for which R.E. and pioneers are required after the assault, and the order in which they should be carried out, are as follows:

(a) The location and construction of strong points.

(*b*) The opening up of communication trenches from our jumping-off trench to the objective.

(*c*) Arrangements for bridging the enemy's trenches, as well as our own jumping-off trench, to enable the field artillery to get forward.

(*d*) Construction of a track for pack transport.

(*e*) Searching for and opening up sources of water supply in the captured position.

(*f*) Providing and fixing signboards and direction marks in the captured trenches.

(*g*) Formation of dumps of R.E. stores near the objective.

(*h*) Repairing and improving dugouts in the captured position for use as command posts.

Also, from the moment the assault starts, a small maintenance party will be required to keep our own trenches clear of obstructions caused by the enemy's shell fire.

The following tasks will normally be dealt with direct by the corps, though at times divisions may be called upon to undertake them. It is unlikely that they can be proceeded with immediately after the assault, although (*i*) is of very great importance.

(*i*) Extension of the tramway system to enable stores to be got forward and wounded evacuated.

(*j*) Repairing roads, leading forward, to take M.T. and heavy guns.

(*k*) Extension of piped water-supply system.

The work required under headings (*a*), (*b*), (*c*), and (*d*) can be determined by previous reconnaissance of the ground and by the study of trench maps and aeroplane photos. The proposed scheme can be shown on sketch maps, which should be issued down to, and including, company commanders of infantry battalions.

5. Taking the tasks given in paragraph 4 above in order:

(*a*) This point has already been dealt with in section 7, paragraph 8. One section of a field company with 25 infantry can construct one of these posts in three to four hours.

(*b*) Pioneers should usually be allotted for this work, together with such Infantry working parties as may be available, the latter working under R.E. supervision.

The opening up of communication across " No Man's Land " is the first consideration; where Russian saps exist this can be quickly done.

The work under this head will include blocking such trenches in the captured position as are not required for communication, in order to prevent troops losing themselves.

(c) This can be done by fixing light wooden bridges, which have been previously made (R.E.), in which case a carrying party will be required; or by ramping or filling in the trenches (pioneers).

(d) This is required where the ground is very much cut up and the roads obliterated by shell fire to enable pack animals with rations and stores to get up to the captured line as soon as possible.

A track 6 feet wide is sufficient, the surface being roughly leveled by filling in the shell holes. The track must be well defined by a double row of posts or pickets, painted white on our side and mud color on the enemy's side. A small ditch, or gutter, on either side is also useful on a dark night in assisting men to keep to the track.

(e) A small party of sappers will be required for this. They should be given any information available as to the water supply in the enemy's lines.

(f) These are required in the captured trenches to enable carrying parties, reliefs, etc., to find their way about.

(g) Some preparation is required for this. Mobile depots of tools and stores, packed on pontoon wagons, can be usefully employed; it may be possible to get them forward the first night. Arrangements must be made to utilize all enemy dumps of R.E. material in the captured position.

(h) Battalion and possibly brigade headquarters will have to move forward, and some dugout accommodation will be required. A detachment of a tunneling company can be usefully employed on this work, if available.

6. The field companies require Infantry carrying parties to work with them. All commanders are averse to weakening their battalions at the eleventh hour by detailing extra-carrying parties. Also, better value will be obtained from these carrying parties if they have had some previous training and are accustomed to work with a particular unit.

It is advisable, therefore, to tell off permanent parties. These parties should join the field companies before the division proceeds to the training area and should remain with them throughout the training and subsequent operations.

It is found that 100 men per field company are sufficient.

7. The time at which the R.E. and pioneer parties should go forward is important.

They must not be allowed to go forward with the assaulting troops, or even to follow them closely. If they do they will inevitably become involved in the fighting and thereby disorganized to a certain extent.

They must be kept back till the situation permits of their proceeding straight to their task; they will then arrive fresh and properly organized, and will be able to get to work at once.

The man on the spot is the only man who can decide when the right moment arrives; he is usually the brigadier of the assaulting brigade; and he must be made responsible for ordering the parties forward. In certain cases it may be found advisable to delegate this responsibility to the battalion commanders in front line.

8. To insure that no time is lost, it is usually best to have the different parties of R.E. and pioneers, who have been allotted tasks in a particular brigade, or battalion, zone of operations, assemble in the vicinity of that brigade or battalion headquarters by zero hour.

The senior officer of all the parties should report to the brigadier, or battalion commander, for information as to when he can commence work.

9. It is important that the field companies and pioneer battalion should take part in all practice assaults of large formations during training.

Their program of work must be drawn up and the actual work must be commenced, although time may not be available to carry it through.

X. Cooperation with Contact Aeroplanes.

1. The instructions for contact patrol work by aeroplanes are attached as Appendix B.

2. This subject must receive attention during training. It has been found that successful cooperation depends entirely on the amount of attention devoted to the subject on the training ground.

Wherever possible the aeroplanes which will work with the division in the actual operations should also work with it during training. An ample supply of flares must be available for training.

3. The points in the instructions to which special attention should be given are as follows:

(*a*) Latter portion of paragraph 1, especially the visit to division or brigade headquarters, prior to going up.

(*b*) Paragraph 2. All ranks must be informed of the special markings, and this point must be included in the instructions (Sec. I, par. 4 (*o*)).

(*c*) Paragraph 4:

> (1) There is still a tendency among commanding officers to imagine that the lighting of flares draws the enemy's artillery fire. It must be thoroughly impressed on all commanding officers that failure to light flares renders their units far more likely to be shelled by our own artillery.
>
> When the supply of flares is plentiful, the absence of flares, when called for by the aeroplane, at any particular point will probably be interpreted by the divisional commander as meaning that our advanced troops have not reached that point, and that he is quite safe in asking for it to be dealt with by artillery if necessary.
>
> (2) It is usually advisable to arrange, and mention in operation orders, the hours at which contact machines will be in the air. This enables the Infantry to be on the lookout for the aeroplane and to have their flares ready. Time is thereby saved, and the aeroplane is not kept waiting unnecessarily in the danger zone.
>
> Experience has shown that a suitable time is half an hour after the scheduled time for reaching the objective at each stage of the operations, with another flight 1½ hours after the scheduled time for reaching the final objective.
>
> (3) It is unnecessary to light flares all along a trench; two or three flares in a bunch every 50 yards is quite sufficient to indicate the line.
>
> (4) The training of battalion and brigade signal personnel in the use of ground signal panels, ground signal strips, and lamps must be completed while the division is in the line and before proceeding to the training area.

During practices on the training ground they must be given as much practice as possible in sending messages to the contact machines.

(*d*) Paragraph 5.

(*e*) Paragraph 6.

(*f*) Table I.

XI. SIGNAL COMMUNICATIONS.

1. The rapid establishment of good signal communications immediately after the assault is one of the most important, though one of the most difficult, things to be dealt with. No possible means of keeping up communication must be neglected.

The O.C. signals of the division must be kept informed of all projected moves and operations, and should attend all staff conferences which concern operations.

Particular attention to the subject during training and careful .preparation before the assault are the best means of insuring success.

Considerations of topography and the siting of our own and hostile trenches will decide the methods which give most promise of success, and on these methods every effort should be concentrated. The parties required for establishing each system must be definitely told off and properly organized beforehand, and should be trained to their particular duties at all rehearsals.

2. *Cable lines for telegraph and telephone.*—(*a*) This is the most valuable form of communication, and every effort must be made to establish the lines securely at the earliest possible moment. To render cable lines reasonably secure requires time and labor, and can only be effected by burying them to a depth of 6 feet or more.

(*b*) The extent to which hastily laid lines on the surface can be kept through depends on the amount of hostile shelling.

Laddered lines are very useful, and can be quickly constructed after the assault.

The vicinity of villages, woods, and roads, which are always heavily shelled, should be avoided as far as possible when selecting cable routes.

Communication trenches in the enemy's line, which will not be required for consolidation, should be previously selected and allotted as cable trenches. The cable can be buried in these, when labor is available, in less time than would be required to dig a new cable trench. The latter is more likely to be noticed than the old communication trench, and, moreover, the communication trench is likely to have dugouts in it which can be used for test points.

(c) Cables must be run out immediately behind the last wave of the assaulting column, the linesmen following a previously selected route. The cable should be carried right through to the trench which is being consolidated, and offices established at points in this trench line which have been previously selected after studying maps and air photographs.

(d) As soon as this has been done efforts must be concentrated on the maintenance of one or two lines leading to important points; it is a waste of time and labor attempting to maintain all the lines. Existing dugouts in the enemy trenches must be told off as test stations on the cable route, and maintenance parties, previously detailed, must be stationed at these test stations.

(e) Special working parties must be placed at the disposal of the O.C. divisional signal company for the purpose of burying the cable across "No Man's Land," and thence forward, via old communication trenches, to the consolidated line. These parties will seldom be able to start work before the night after the assault.

(f) Where Russian saps have been run out it may be possible to get the cable part of the way across "No Man's Land " before the assault by laying the cable at the bottom of the sap; then, when the roof of the sap is broken in, the cable will be buried sufficiently to protect it from shrapnel and also from traffic in the sap.

3. *Visual.*—Where the topography of the ground is suitable good results can be obtained with visual.

(a) This system depends more than any other on previous preparation; all details must be worked out, points where it is proposed to establish stations in the enemy's lines being approximately located by reconnaissance and by the study of maps. In this connection enemy machine-gun emplacements have been found valuable. When completed the scheme, with a sketch map, must be issued to all concerned.

Back stations in our own lines must be specially prepared and provided with overhead cover.

(b) A selected officer, either of the Signal Service or an officer in charge of battalion signals, should be placed in charge of the organization, and he should be given the N.C.O.'s, signalers, and equipment required to work the scheme. It will usually be necessary to call on battalions to find the necessary personnel.

(c) Each signal station to be established in the enemy's lines should be allotted to a definite battalion. The personnel detailed for each station will assemble at the battalion headquarters prior to the assault and will be sent forward by the battalion commander as soon as the objective has been gained. They should not be sent over with the assaulting columns.

The personnel should be lightly equipped; they must carry the signaling equipment fastened to the person in as inconspicuous a manner as possible, while yet leaving them free to use their weapons if necessary.

(d) The signalers of assaulting companies move with the company commander and should carry signaling shutters for the purpose of getting into communication with their own unit as soon as the objective has been reached and before the main visual scheme has been established.

Lamps should be reserved for the main scheme; they are too bulky to be carried in the assault and also are difficult to replace.

(e) All visual signalers need special training to give them confidence in repeating a message several times to a known back station which may not be able to reply forward; it is most desirable, however, that the back stations should acknowledge whenever possible.

4. *Pigeons.*—These are invaluable when properly organized and used.

Attention is drawn to "Notes on the use of carrier pigeons," S.S. 123.

The pigeons and personnel available must be definitely allotted to the different units and arrangements must be made for maintaining the supply of pigeons.

At the commencement of the assault the pigeons and pigeon men must be kept back at battalion headquarters and sent forward as soon as the position has been gained. The men must be given definite orders as to whom they are to report to and must be provided with a guide if necessary.

In the front line pigeons must be kept in dugouts to protect them from shell fire, mud, and wet as much as possible.

Pigeons should be reserved for important messages; all officers should be instructed how to write clear and concise messages in the pigeon-message book.

5. *Wireless.*—Attention is called to " Notes on Wireless," S.S. 100.

(*a*) A wireless set, placed at the disposal of a division by the corps, must be allotted to a definite commander or to a specially appointed officer, who will be responsible for deciding what messages are to be sent by wireless and for arranging for the messages to be coded.

(*b*) Wireless should be reserved for urgent messages, such as calls for barrage fire, etc,; the message must be short and concise, to facilitate coding and decoding.

(*c*) At the commencement of an assault a wireless set should not, as a rule, be in advance of brigade headquarters; but as soon as the position has been gained a wireless set should be sent forward to a selected battalion headquarters or to a selected position if the site of battalion headquarters is not suitable.

(*d*) A commander ordering a wireless set to move forward will arrange for:

(1) Written orders as to whom the party are to report to and at whose disposal the set is to be placed.

(2) A carrying party of six men.

(3) A guide to the new position.

(*e*) As far as possible the points to which the wireless sets are to move forward must be decided on before the assault and notified to all commanders concerned; otherwise the latter will be unaware of the existence of wireless communication in the forward area and will consequently not make use of it.

(*f*) It is impossible to obtain good results from the delicate wireless instruments unless the set is installed in a reasonably dry dugout, which should be reserved for wireless only. Heavily shelled areas must be avoided, otherwise the difficulty of maintaining the aerial may render the set useless.

6. *Earth induction sets.*—Some of these sets may also be placed at the disposal of a division by the corps.

The same conditions as laid down for wireless apply to the use of these sets.

The forward stations, which can send only, will usually be worked by battalion signalers, who must be specially trained in the use of the power buzzer which is employed.

The back stations will be worked by the corps wireless personnel; dugout accommodation near the head of the buried cable will be required for these stations.

7. Runners.—This is the one means of communication which can be relied on when all other means fail; and, therefore, commanders must devote great care to the training and organization of their runners. Company runners must be trained with their companies.

Opinions vary as to the actual number required; the following has been found to be a good average number:

At battalion headquarters, 10 men; 2 of these are detailed particularly as brigade runners, and 2 from each company to work primarily, but not solely, between their own company and battalion headquarters.

At company headquarters, 4 men.

Each platoon commander also requires a runner; his servant is the most satisfactory man.

Runners should be lightly equipped and should wear a distinctive mark; they should be young, lightly built, and intelligent. Every man must be thoroughly familiar with *all* the routes to *all* the principal centers within their battalion sector, i. e., to *all* company headquarters, and not only to their own, to *all* forward dumps, to the headquarters of battalions on the flanks, to the headquarters of the brigade, and to the advanced report center.

It must be impressed upon all runners that the quicker they go the safer they are.

Company and platoon runners must go forward with their respective commanders.

Runners must be sent in turn and must be rested as far as possible when not actually at work. A small supply of rum should be kept for them when the work is hard.

Where messages have to be carried a long distance, e. g., to brigades, some arrangement of relays is required. The establishment of a brigade advanced report center well forward, at the head of the buried cable, if existing, is useful; a N.C.O. of the brigade signal section should be in charge there. Battalion runners will bring their messages to this point, whence the contents can be telephoned to brigade headquarters, the actual messages themselves being sent on by special brigade runners.

Relay posts may often be required between brigade headquarters and advanced divisional headquarters, or perhaps between the reserve brigade headquarters and headquarters of brigades in front line. Every relay post must be labeled and numbered.

Mounted orderlies are also useful for communication between advanced divisional headquarters and brigade headquarters; a troop of corps Cavalry, if available, is most useful for this work.

On no account should any verbal messages be sent by runners; every message must be in writing. Verbal messages should generally be ignored.

8. *Artillery messages.*—Company and battalion commanders of assaulting units must be prepared to assist F.O.O.'s and Artillery liaison officers in getting their messages back.

The Artillery can not always provide sufficient runners for their forward officers; and, where it is not possible to keep a line open owing to shelling, an Infantry runner will often be the only means of getting an Artillery message through.

There must be the closest cooperation between the signal service of the division and the Artillery as regards the transmission of Artillery messages; and, in deciding on the means of communication to be established, the needs of the Artillery must be considered and provided for as far as possible, particularly in the buried cable routes forward from our jumping-off trenches.

9. *Accommodation for signal personnel.*—The efficient working and maintenance of communications depends largely on the accommodation available for the personnel engaged in working them.

Commanders must not forget this point when establishing headquarters in a captured position. If signalers, pigeon men, wireless operators, and runners are all crowded together in one small dugout, it is difficult for them to maintain good communications.

XII. SITUATION REPORTS.

All subordinate commanders are responsible for keeping their respective superiors, as well as neighboring commanders, regularly informed of the progress of events and of important changes in the situation as they occur. (Field Service Regulations, Pt. I, sec. 8 (2).)

1. *Situation reports.*—The great importance of this is not always realized by company and battalion commanders; the failure to keep superiors informed of the situation, both of our own troops and of the enemy, is a fault which is chiefly due to lack of training. Therefore training must be carried on till

officers can be relied upon to render their reports automatically, even in the heat of an action.

Even in many cases where situation reports are sent in, the report is often so loosely or badly worded that it is difficult for the recipient to gather its correct meaning. The art of writing, or dictating, clear, concise reports can only be acquired by constant practice. Long, rambling messages merely serve to block the wires.

It must not be forgotten that negative reports or information are just as important as positive.

The use of the telephone is largely responsible for these inferior reports; it should be a rule in every formation that telephone messages are only verbal messages and therefore should, when possible, be confirmed either by written message or telegram.

It is often quicker, especially for commanders in the front line, to send in rough sketches instead of writing a long message. The groundwork for these sketches can be prepared in a notebook before the attack commences; this groundwork is really a rough copy of that portion of the trench map covering the ground over which the unit will be working. It need not be drawn to scale as long as the boundary lines of the squares are clearly marked.

When the commander wishes to send in his report, he has only to mark up his own position, that of the nearest enemy, and of the units on his flanks, as far as known. This will not take a minute and it will be perfectly clear to the recipient.

2. *Reconnaissance by staff officers.*—Although it is the duty of subordinate commanders to keep their superiors informed of the situation this does not relieve superiors of the responsibility of obtaining the earliest possible information as to the situation by every means in their power.

To effect this the fullest use must be made of staff officers, who must be sent to ascertain the situation both of our own and of the enemy's troops and the general conditions prevailing in the forward area.

All officers of the staff, both administrative and personal, as well as the General Staff, are available for this work.

Where communications have entirely broken down, personal reconnaissance by staff officers is the quickest and surest method of ascertaining the situation.

Officers of higher formations working on the ground should always report after reconnaissance to the commanders of the troops they have visited in order to afford the latter any information they have acquired and to adjust their own impressions by the views of the man on the spot.

3. *Liaison between division and brigade.*—Where he considers it necessary, the divisional commander should detail a responsible staff officer to act as liaison officer with a brigade in front line. The duty of this officer will be to keep the divisional commander informed of the situation as known at brigade headquarters, to assist the brigade staff, and to see that the intentions of the divisional commander are correctly interpreted by brigades.

4. *Observers.*—The use of special observers, posted in positions from which they can watch the progress of the assault, is one means by which commanders can get early information as to the situation.

These observers may be either staff officers or specially selected officers or men; in the latter cases they will require special training; they must also be fully acquainted with the ground and with the details of the plan of attack.

They should be in direct telephonic communication, if possible by buried cable, with their headquarters, and their observation posts should be proof against shrapnel at least.

If it can be arranged, a position on the flank of the assault is best, as the view in that case is not so liable to be obstructed by the hostile barrage.

5. *Information from wounded.*—Another method by which information as to the situation may be obtained is to post an officer of the brigade staff at the advanced report center (see sec. 11, par. 7), where he can get in touch with wounded officers and men coming back and find out the situation from them. At times valuable information may be obtained by this method, but too much reliance must not be placed on the statements of a wounded man.

6. *Flank liaison officers.*—To insure that neighboring commanders are kept regularly informed as to the progress of events, liaison officers (or N.C.O.'s in the case of battalions if an officer is not available) must be exchanged by all assaulting brigades and battalions with the corresponding brigade or battalion on either flank.

When good communications exist between divisions, the exchange of liaison officers is usually unnecessary, provided the divisional commander has an officer at his headquarters whom he can send to neighboring divisional headquarters whenever he wishes to obtain or explain the situation.

The duty of a liaison officer is to keep his own commander constantly informed of the progress and situation of the unit with whom he is in liaison. Every liaison officer must be provided by his own unit with some means of communication.

XIII. Movement of Headquarters.

1. *Divisional headquarters.*—As a rule the divisional report center should not move during the operations, when the task allotted is a limited objective. The disadvantages of the dislocation of the signal communications, caused by a forward move, will usually outweigh the advantages of being a mile or two nearer the firing line.

This does not prevent the divisional commander and his staff going forward to ascertain the situation at any time during the action.

Previous arrangements must, however, be made for a move forward in case the enemy collapses, and the necessary accommodation must be prepared; as a general rule, the new position should be somewhere on the buried cable route.

2. *Brigade headquarters.*—(*a*) In the case of a front line brigade, detailed to capture the first two objectives, it will not be necessary for the headquarters to move as a rule; the advanced report center (sec. 11, par. 7) should, however, be moved forward to the vicinity of the first objective after the capture of the second, in order to lighten the work of the runners of the units who have captured the second objective.

(*b*) In the case of a second-line brigade, detailed to capture a third or fourth objective, a move forward will be necessary to enable the brigadier to keep in touch with his battalion commanders.

The best way of arranging this appears to be as follows:

The brigade orderly officer, with a small party of scouts and signalers, should go forward as soon as the first objective has been gained and should select a suitable spot in the vicinity of the first objective; he then sends back word to his brigade and also to a party of signalers, specially detailed, who should be waiting at the head of the buried cable, telling them the position selected.

The brigadier then notifies all concerned as to where he will establish his headquarters; in the meantime the signalers run out a line to the selected spot from the head of the buried cable.

When his brigade moves forward to pass through the troops engaged in consolidating the first and second objectives, the brigadier moves straight to the selected headquarters, which the orderly officer should by that time have been able to render fit for occupation. A small party of sappers placed at the latter's disposal can be usefully employed in this work. (See Sec. IX, par. 4 (*h*).)

3. *Battalion headquarters.*—(*a*) In the assault on the first objective the C.O. has nothing to gain by moving forward with his battalion and should not be allowed to do so. He must, however, keep in close touch with the progress of the assault by means of special observers and must be ready to take charge at once if the assault is checked.

His headquarters should not move forward till the objective has been gained, and even then it must wait till the new position has been selected and the route to it reconnoitered before vacating the old position.

(*b*) In the case of a unit detailed for the assault of a second or subsequent objective, the C.O. must move forward with his unit as far as the furthest objective already captured and establish his headquarters in that vicinity; whether he himself continues to go forward with the battalion or not depends on the situation; but in· any case he must establish his headquarters in some place where runners can find it.

The selection of this new position and the notification of it should be carried out in the same manner as advocated in paragraph 2 (*b*) above.

4. *Notification of movement.*—When a commander is about to move his headquarters, notification must be sent to all commanders with whom he is in communication, both above, below, and to the flanks, telling them that he is about to move and the position to which he is moving. Similarly, on arrival at his new position, he must inform all concerned of the fact.

Failure in this respect means the miscarriage of orders, delay, etc., and has in some cases been responsible for the failure of the operation.

5. *Movements of commanders.*—Whenever a commander leaves his headquarters he must leave information as to where he is going and what route he proposes to follow, in order that runners with urgent messages may be able to find him.

Also, whenever he is absent from his headquarters, he must arrange to leave a responsible officer in charge; this latter must know the commander's intentions, in order to be able to deal with situations which may arise during the latter's absence.

XIV. ACTION OF TANKS.

1. In the present stage of their development, tanks must be regarded as entirely accessory to the ordinary methods of attack, i. e., to the advance of Infantry in close cooperation with the Artillery.

Any modifications or alterations required in the plan of attack, when tanks are employed, must be such as will not jeopardize the success of the attack in the event of a failure by the tanks.

2. The ideal to be aimed at in planning the action of the tanks is that they should reach the enemy's trenches just ahead of the Infantry, but not more than 50 yards ahead, otherwise they will run into our own barrage. The barrage must not be altered for the tanks.

When this is not possible the tanks should follow up the Infantry as closely as possible and be ready to deal with any strong points, machine guns, or wire which may be holding up the Infantry.

3. The ideal is difficult to attain for the following reasons:

(*a*) Owing to the noise, it has not been found possible to approach the tanks nearer than 400 yards from the enemy's line without risk of discovery. Where our jumping-off trench is within 200 yards of the enemy, the tank will therefore have to start 200 yards behind the leading wave.

(*b*) Any attempt to overcome the difficulty in (*a*) by starting the tanks before zero will bring down the enemy's barrage earlier, with the result that our Infantry may not get started at all.

(*c*) The pace at which the tank can travel over bad ground, cut up by shell fire and intersected by trenches, will not enable it to catch up and pass the Infantry, when both start at zero, before the latter reach the enemy's trenches.

4. Unless the ground is very favorable for the movement of the tanks, it is better not to attempt the ideal, but to be content with letting the tanks follow the Infantry as closely as they can, ready to help them if they get into difficulties.

5. In this case a careful study of the ground, maps, and air photographs will indicate the points at which trouble is most likely to occur, and the line of advance of each tank can be then worked out, so as to bring them as near as possible to these points. Tanks, however, must not adhere rigidly to the line of advance laid down, but must be prepared to go wherever their services are needed. As a rule, tanks should always be employed by sections of four.

6. To insure successful action the most careful reconnaissance of the ground by each tank officer is necessary; this should be carried out in company with the C.O. of the battalion in whose zone of attack the tank will be working, in order that the tank officer may see the points at which the C.O. anticipates trouble.

In addition each tank officer must be given every facility of studying maps and air photographs to enable him to become absolutely familiar with the ground. Roads, wet ground, and ground badly cut up by shell fire should be avoided where possible.

7. Special instructions must be issued to each tank officer as to what part he is to play in the assault. These instructions must be as clear and as detailed as it is possible to make them.

8. *The approach march.*—The task of getting the tanks into position for the assault is by no means easy; careful preparations and reconnaissance are required.

Normally the tanks move forward to a position of assembly, where they fill up with petrol, etc., and make any final adjustments needed. From this point to the position of deployment the tanks must always move under cover of darkness. Commanders must be prepared to assist tanks in the move to the position of deployment by providing guides, either officers or scouts, by laying down tapes to mark the route, and, where the ground is very cut up by shell holes, by filling these in and making a rough track for the tank to follow. To drown the noise during the latter portion of the move it may be necessary to keep up machine-gun fire or shelling.

The officer of each tank must reconnoiter his route, in company with the guides detailed to help him, both by day and night.

Zero hour must be communicated to each tank officer before he leaves the position of assembly, where also the final synchronization of watches must be carried out. A staff officer should be detailed for this duty and to supervise the arrangements for getting the tanks into position.

9. *Pace.*—The speed of tanks of the original type is approximately as follows:

By night, 15 yards a minute.

By day, over ground badly cut up by shell fire, 15 yards a minute.

By day, over ground not badly cut up by shell fire and over ordinary trenches, 30 yards a minute.

By day, on open ground, 90 yards a minute.

Tanks can cross any wire entanglement, and they leave a track which is passable by Infantry. The wire is not, however, in any way removed, and loose strands remain on the ground, which may act as trip wires. Tanks can push their way through brushwood, but can not negotiate woods containing trees of any size.

When moving through a village they must keep to the roads; if they attempt to cross ruins, they are liable to fall into cellars or dugouts.

10. *Signals.*—The following signals have proved useful:

From tanks to Infantry: Red flag—Am broken down. Green flag—Am on my objective.

From Infantry to tanks: " Enemy in sight " signal with rifle—tanks required here.

Pigeons have also been used with success from tanks.

XV. USE OF SMOKE BOMBS AND CLOUD GAS.

1. The discharge of gas and smoke, or of smoke alone, is regarded by the enemy as a prelude to the assault, and usually draws his barrage on to the trenches from which the discharges are issuing.

This fact may be taken advantage of during the preliminary bombardment to enable the general lie of the enemy's barrage to be ascertained, and thereby to enable arrangements to be made to avoid casualties when the assault takes place.

If smoke is used just before the assault to conceal the advance, the risk of the assaulting troops losing direction and of bringing down the enemy's barrage prematurely must be taken into account. It can, however, be usefully employed on those portic⸗

of the front from which no assault is taking place to draw the enemy's barrage fire away from the front of assault. ·

2. Smoke bombs can be used on the front of assault during the advance for special purposes, viz:

(*a*) To blind any machine guns likely to cause trouble by enfilade fire.

(*b*) To conceal the advance of reserves.

Attention is drawn to S.S. 130, " Notes on employment of 4-inch Stokes mortar bombs."

3. As regards (*a*), this is especially effective on the flanks of the attack.

The smoke barrage must start at zero, and fire should be as rapid as possible to insure the smoke screen being formed before the enemy has time to discover our advance.

4. As regards (*b*), smoke can be employed where reserves, detailed for the assault of a later objective, have to cross a long stretch of open ground, exposed to view by the enemy, between our jumping-off trenches and the line already gained by our troops.

To effect this the mortars must be sent forward as soon as possible after the first objective has been captured, in order to give them time to establish themselves in a forward position and to get up the necessary ammunition.

A carrying party must be detailed beforehand to assist the detachments.

5. Where possible the detachments of the special brigade, which will be working with the division in the assault, should be present during the training, and should actually practice the barrages required in order that the troops, especially in (*b*), may be given practice in advancing through the smoke without losing direction.

XVI. MACHINE GUNS.

Attention is drawn to S.S. 106, " Notes on the tactical employment of machine guns and Lewis guns," and to S.S. 122, " Some notes on Lewis guns and machine guns."

1. The duties which fall to machine guns in the attack are:

(*a*) To provide covering fire for the attacking Infantry.

(*b*) To cover the withdrawal of the Infantry in case the attack fails.

(*c*) To fill up gaps which may occur in the assaulting line.

(*d*) To assist in consolidation of position won and to repel counter-attacks.

2. *Covering fire.*—The power which the present number of machine guns in a division places in the hands of the divisional commander is not always fully realized.

Without in any way reducing the number of guns required to provide for (*b*), (*c*), and (*d*) above, there are now sufficient guns in a division to supply covering fire, similar to the artillery barrage, along the whole divisional front.

Where the ground admits, direct fire should be always used, but if this is not possible, excellent results can be obtained by indirect fire, provided careful arrangements have been made beforehand.

The arrangements for the barrage for the whole corps front may be coordinated by the corps machine-gun officer, under the orders of the corps commander, but the control of the barrage on each divisional front must be entirely in the hands of the divisional commander immediately the attack starts.

Such guns of attacking brigades as are used for covering fire must remain under the orders of their own brigadier, so that he can apply their fire where it is required as the attack progresses.

The guns of the divisional machine-gun company, and a portion of the guns of the reserve brigades, can be kept under divisional control at the outset and used for covering or barrage fire on communication trenches, forming-up places for reserves and concealed lines of approach and to assist in the howitzer bombardment. (Sec. III, par. 4 (*b*).)

The lifts of the barrage must be carefully worked out to synchronize with the movement of the Artillery barrage and, where indirect fire is being used, the barrage must be kept at least 400 yards ahead of the Infantry.

When the objective has been gained, the machine-gun barrage conforms to the movements of the Artillery barrage as regards ceasing and commencing fire; it should usually be employed to barrage covered lines of approach, and places where the enemy might assemble for the counterattack.

To obtain the best results all groups of guns employed for covering fire and barrage work should be linked up with the buried cable system.

One belt per gun per four minutes has been found to be a satisfactory average rate of fire for a sustained barrage.

3. *Guns to cover a withdrawal.*—These guns are required to hold our front-line trenches in case the assault fails at the outset.

As a rule one section per brigade front will be found sufficient.

Once the attack has reached its objective the guns will be available for other duties.

4. *Guns to fill gaps.*—With the number of Lewis guns now at the disposal of the battalion commander, he should usually be able to retain sufficient Lewis guns in his own hands for this purpose without requiring the assistance of machine guns.

Where, however, a brigade commander considers it necessary, he may allot one or two machine guns from his machine-gun company to each assaulting battalion to be at the disposal of the C.O. for filling gaps which may occur in his line during the assault.

These guns should not be sent forward with the assaulting column, but should be kept in hand until it is seen where they are required.

5. *Guns to assist in consolidation.*—The guns referred to in paragraph 4 will be available for this duty, but other guns will be required for use in the strong points. (Sec. VII, par. 8 (*b*).)

These latter guns will not be sent forward for an hour or two after the assault, and therefore are available at the outset for other duties. The simplest way would probably be to use them as in paragraph 3 at the commencement of the action.

6. *Relief of gunners.*—The necessity for keeping a proportion of gunners out of the fight, both for the purpose of replacing casualties and of relieving the men in action, must not be forgotten.

This is especially necessary in the case of guns detailed for barrage work; the nervous strain of maintaining fire for a long period tells very heavily on the detachments.

It may be necessary, therefore, to provide men from battalions to assist the machine-gun company, especially in the work of carrying up belt boxes and ammunition supply generally.

7. *Action of machine-gun company commander.*—The various tasks which his company has to carry out demand the most careful preparation and organization on the part of the company commander.

He must insure that all section commanders fully understand the part they have to play, and he must be always on the watch to regain control, at the earliest possible moment, of any guns temporarily detached, as in paragraph 4, in order to provide a reserve for his brigade commander.

8. *Action of machine guns before the attack.*—Night firing, during the preliminary bombardment, on the enemy's dumps, transport roads, etc., is important, and must be provided for. (See Sec. III, par. 3 (*e*).)

XVII. Lewis Guns.

Attention is drawn to S.S. 106 and S.S. 122.

1. The action of Lewis guns must be considered under three separate headings, viz:

(*a*) Before the assault.

(*b*) During the assault.

(*c*) After the assault.

2. *Before the assault.*—Great value can be obtained from Lewis guns at this stage, if properly handled, in knocking out hostile machine guns. A few guns should be pushed out into " No Man's Land " under cover of darkness or fog and established in shell holes, as near as possible, without interfering with the 18-pounder barrage, to the enemy's front trench.

At zero these guns open fire on any known enemy machine-gun emplacements in the front trench, or in " No Man's Land," and also assist the 18-pounder barrage in keeping the enemy's Infantry down by sweeping his parapet; they maintain this fire until it is masked by the advance of the Infantry. They then cease fire and wait till the Infantry have captured the front-line trench before following up the assaulting column.

Should the attack fail to get into the front-line trench, they must maintain their positions and endeavor to silence any enemy machine guns which are holding up the attack.

As the enemy machine guns always use enfilade fire, the Lewis guns must do the same if they are to be successful.

3. *During the assault.*—(*a*) If the attack goes through without a check, Lewis guns are not required with the leading lines; but in order to give the leading troops some means of dealing with machine guns which may have escaped the bombardment and barrage Lewis guns must be close at hand.

The selection of the exact position for the guns in the assaulting columns should be left to battalion commanders; as a rule it has been found convenient for the guns of each assaulting company to move on the flanks of the second wave. In this position they are to a certain extent screened from view by the leading wave and yet are not too far back if wanted.

(*b*) The question of Lewis guns with mopping-up parties needs consideration. Normally the rifle, with the bayonet and bomb for close quarters, should be sufficient. Where, however, long stretches of communication trenches have to be cleared, Lewis guns will be required to support the bombers.

(*c*) The C.O. will require some guns to fill up gaps in his line during the assault. Some of the guns of his reserve companies could be made available for this. They can either be sent forward with the reserve or kept back in the C.O.'s hands. (See sec. XVI, par. 4.) In any case the detachments must be clearly instructed as to their rôle.

4. *After the assault.*—(*a*) Lewis guns are required for three purposes :

(1) For the outpost line.   (Sec. VII, par. 4 (*b*).)

(2) To back up patrols exploiting success.   (Sec. VIII, par. 3.)

(3) To garrison the line which is being consolidated.

(*b*) As regards (1) and (2), the duties of these guns have already been discussed.

As regards (3), a certain number of guns are required for this line, in addition to those in the outpost line, in order that the garrison may be thinned out after consolidation to the number of men for whom reasonable cover from shell fire is available.

(*c*) In view of the number of tasks to be carried out, the guns must be allotted to them previous to the assault, otherwise there is certain to be confusion and loss of time.

It would appear to be simplest to allot (1) and (3) to the guns of the assaulting companies, and (2) to the guns of the reserve companies. These latter guns will have time to get up to the front, ready to go forward, while the barrage is dying down.

5. *Size of detachments.*—Two men only are required to work a Lewis gun, and not more than two trained gunners per gun should be allowed to go forward with the assault.

The rest of the detachment must be kept back ; otherwise there is a chance of one shell knocking out the whole trained detachment.

The carrying forward of ammunition must be done by men specially detailed.

6. *Ammunition supply.*—It is advisable not to send more than half the authorized number of magazines forward with each gun at the outset, the remainder being stored in some convenient dugout near the jumping-off line, under charge of a party of spare gunners, who would be available to replace casualties. As

the magazines with the guns are emptied they can be sent back by the carriers to the reserve and exchanged for full ones, the empty ones being refilled by the spare gunners.

This method is preferable to that of taking all the magazines forward at the outset, as then the empty magazines, being left lying about in shell holes, etc., get smashed, mislaid, and full of mud or grit.

7. *Care of the gun.*—Some form of cover, capable of being removed instantaneously, is essential for each gun. The cover should be kept on the gun during the assault and until the gun actually opens fire.

Without this mud or grit will get into the gun and put it out of action.

XVIII. Action of Snipers.

1. To obtain the fullest value from snipers armed with telescopic-sighted rifles, particular attention must be paid to their training for the different tasks which they have to carry out in addition to their training as sharpshooters.

Like Lewis guns, snipers can be employed before, during, and after the assault.

2. *Before the assault.*—Snipers have two tasks to perform:

(a) To prevent the enemy observing our trenches and thus detecting signs that an assault is impending. Our snipers must obtain complete mastery of the situation and force the enemy to keep under cover.

(b) To establish themselves in shell holes, etc., well forward in "No Man's Land," in positions from which they can deal with hostile machine guns, especially those pushed out in front of the enemy's trenches and which have been located by the patrols.

3. *During the assault.*—(a) Immediately the barrage commences the snipers in "No Man's Land" must endeavor first to pick off the detachments of any known enemy machine guns in conjunction with the Lewis guns, and then turn their attention to the garrison of the trench, particularly the officers, before the advance of the Infantry masks their fire.

(b) Men armed with telescopic-sighted rifles should not go forward with the assaulting column. It is better to keep them back until the objective has been gained and then send them forward; otherwise there is a risk of the men becoming casualties and the telescopic sights, which are difficult to replace, being lost.

4. *After the assault.*—(*a*) Immediately after the objective has been gained selected good shots in each company should take up a position on the old enemy parapet of the captured trench. From this vantage ground they will be able to fire over the heads of the Infantry consolidating the trench, and will be able to command the enemy's line beyond, particularly the communication trenches running forward. Where these men have been previously detailed, and when they take up their position at once, they will be able to do considerable execution among the retreating enemy and to increase his demoralization; often they will be able to assist in breaking up an immediate counterattack by picking off the leaders.

In the meantime the snipers with their telescopic-sighted rifles will be coming forward and establishing posts in the captured line.

(*b*) Where bombing blocks have been established in communication trenches, a pair of snipers, established in rear of the block where they can enfilade it, will be of great assistance in repulsing bombing counterattacks up the trench. (See VII, par. 4 (*c*)).

XIX. PATROLS AND SCOUTS.

1. The importance of training in patrol work must be impressed on all commanders; it is not always realized how important good patrol work is, especially after the enemy's original defenses have been broken through and when the fighting is becoming more like open warfare.

2. *Before the assault.*—The duties of patrols at this stage are:

(*a*) Obtaining complete command of "No Man's Land." This is of special importance, especially from the point of view of morale, both for cultivating an offensive spirit and for the resulting feeling of confidence created among the troops about to attack.

The larger the number of men who have been "over the top" on patrols, the greater the confidence of the unit.

Command of "No Man's Land" is also necessary in order to prevent the enemy detecting Russian saps and other preparations for the assault.

Before night advances can be made complete command of "No Man's Land" is essential.

(*b*) Ascertaining and reporting upon the damage done by the Artillery bombardment, especially with reference to wire cutting and the destruction of certain special points.

(c) Locating enemy machine guns and snipers pushed out into " No Man's Land " in front of their trenches, and reporting these positions. (Sec. XVIII, par. 2 (b).)

3. *After the assault.*—Patrols are required:

(a) As *battle patrols* to follow up the retreating enemy and to seize tactical features temporarily unoccupied by the enemy beyond the line already gained by the Infantry. This point has been fully dealt with in Section VIII, paragraph 3.

(b) As *reconnoitering patrols* to locate the enemy's new position and to obtain information as to the ground between that position and our most advanced line. This work should be undertaken by the battalion scouts.

The scouts detailed for this work should not accompany the assault, but should move up as soon as the objective has been taken. They then work their way forward in small parties, using such cover as may be obtainable, till they have succeeded in locating the enemy's line.

They must take note of the ground traversed, what obstacles there are to movement, wire, etc., and covered lines of approach. One man must then return to his C.O. with the report, the rest of the party remaining in observation of the enemy.

4. *Guides.*—In addition to their duties in 3 (b), the scouts will be required to act as guides for carrying parties, reconnoitering officers, troops coming up to relieve or to pass through their own unit.

XX. Action of Stokes Mortars.

1. The action of Stokes mortars can be considered in three different phases of the assault:

(a) Immediately after zero and until the barrage lifts from the enemy's front trench.

(b) During the remainder of the advance.

(c) After the objective has been captured, i. e., during consolidation.

2. *Immediately after zero.*—(a) Stokes mortars can be used to supplement, or thicken up, the 18-pounder barrage on the front or support trenches, their fire being directed especially against machine-gun emplacements, or any strong point which requires extra treatment.

(b) They must conform to the movements of the 18-pounder barrage, commencing at zero and lifting in accordance with the Artillery program.

(*c*) Success in this phase is inspired by good emplacements, careful registration, and an ample dump of ammunition.

(*d*) Should the assault fail to reach the enemy front trench, the Stokes mortars must at once reopen fire on the enemy trench and machine-gun emplacements, and continue this fire until the Artillery bombardment is recommenced.

3. *During the advance.*—(*a*) Once the Infantry have crossed the enemy's front line the Stokes mortars must be moved forward before they can be employed again.

(*b*) The task for which they are best suited and for which they will most often be required in this stage of the assault is that of dealing with any enemy machine guns, or strong points, which may be temporarily holding up part of our advance.

(*c*) If a Stokes mortar can be got up into position, a short hurricane bombardment for not more than two minutes, followed by a determined rush with the bayonet, will usually succeed in overcoming the opposition, and thus enable the advance to be resumed. During this bombardment the party detailed to attack must work forward as far as possible, in order to be ready to rush in the instant the bombardment lifts.

(*d*) For this purpose it will usually be advisable to place one or two mortars at the disposal of each assaulting battalion. These mortars must move forward with the assaulting column, usually immediately in rear of it, but they must not advance too far; if they do, it will be difficult to find them when they are wanted. The best plan appears to be to send them forward to some prearranged rendezvous, previously notified to all concerned, in the enemy's front or support line. Any company requiring their assistance would then be able to find them quickly.

(*e*) The officer in charge of these mortars must endeavor to keep in touch with the situation as far as possible, and must be ready to move forward to the assistance of any party whom he may see to be hung up without waiting to be sent for.

(*f*) While the Stokes mortars are being brought up and got into position, the senior Infantry officer on the spot must be collecting his men and making arrangements for the assault, so that no time may be lost once the mortars are in position.

(*g*) The cooperation between Infantry and Stokes mortars in situations of this nature can be greatly improved by practice, and as much practice as possible should be given during training.

4. *After the assault.*—As soon as the objective has been captured some mortars must be sent up and established in rear of

any blocks which have been formed in communication trenches running forward from the line which is being consolidated.

Here they will be of great value in assisting the bombers holding the block to repulse enemy bombing attacks up the trench.

5. *Distribution of mortars.*—The Stokes mortar battery of a brigade attacking with two battalions in first line might be distributed as follows:

(*a*) *During first phase.*—All mortars in action in vicinity of our front-line trenches (see par. 2).

(*b*) *During second phase.*—All mortars follow up advancing columns immediately to prearranged rendezvous in enemy's front or support trenches; two mortars in rear of each assaulting battalion (see par. 3); remainder to some central point, under the battery commander. This enables the mortars to be got across "No Man's Land" before the enemy barrage comes down.

(*c*) *During third phase.*—The four mortars under the battery commander move forward and establish themselves in the consolidated line (see par. 4).

Meanwhile the battery commander must regain control of his detached mortars, whose task should be finished, and reorganize them with a view to sending them forward again in support of the reserve battalions of the brigade, passing through to capture the second objective.

6. *Ammunition supply.*—Each mortar when moving forward requires a carrying party of 10 Infantrymen to assist the detachment in carrying ammunition and in keeping up the supply between the mortars and the dumps. These are in addition to the carrying parties required to form the dumps.

7. *Cooperation with bombers.*—Stokes mortars must always be used in bombing attacks to barrage behind the enemy bombers, and to prevent reenforcements of men and bombs reaching the enemy.

During the assault mortars should not, as a rule, be required for this duty, though where the moppers-up have to deal with long stretches of communication trenches a Stokes mortar may be attached to them with advantage.

XXI. Action of Medium Trench Mortars.

The action of medium trench mortars for wire cutting and bombardment during the preliminary bombardment is included in the corps Artillery plan.

Once the assault has commenced, the medium trench mortars are usually not required.

One or two mortars may, however, be found useful in dealing with machine guns in concrete emplacements, strong points, or wire, which may have checked part of the advance, and which Stokes mortars have failed to deal with.

For this purpose it has been found convenient to organize an improvised mobile section of two mortars, in a limbered G.S. wagon, or possibly on pack animals, which can be sent forward to wherever their services are required.

The ammunition will usually have to be sent up by hand, the whole of the available gunners from the medium and heavy batteries being pooled for this purpose, so as to avoid calling on the Infantry for carrying parties.

Owing to the unwieldly nature and weight of the equipment and ammunition, and the number of men required to handle them, these mortars will seldom be able to go forward before dark. But officers must be sent forward to reconnoiter the position in daylight and ascertain the situation, as soon as it is known where they are required, in order that no time may be lost in reconnaissance when the mortars arrive.

When the mortars are in position, the bombardment must be deliberate and must be continued until the obstruction has been demolished.

XXII. Action of Bombers.

Attention is drawn to S.S. 126, " The Training and Employment of Bombers."

1. At the present time there is a great danger of the importance of the bomb being unduly emphasized at the expense of the rifle and bayonet. It must be impressed on all ranks that the rifle and bayonet is, and always will be, the Infantryman's principal weapons, and that they can not be too familiar with them or too expert in their use.

2. Attacks over the open with the rifle and bayonet, if vigorously pushed home, will always succeed in making progress when the cooperation between the Infantry and Artillery is good. Bombing attacks along trenches, however vigorous and however well supported by Artillery, will never succeed in making any real progress. It may be taken for granted that once an attack has come down to the bombing stage the operation has come to a standstill.

3. There are, however, three duties for which bombers are required during an assault, and for which they must be trained, viz:

(a). To assist the moppers-up in clearing out and capturing the garrisons of trenches already passed over by the assaulting waves.

(b) To assist in holding the captured position by repulsing enemy bombing attacks.

(c) To assist in gaining touch, after the objective has been reached, with units on the flanks, by clearing out any enemy who may be still holding out in the objective between their own unit and the unit on the flank.

4. *Assisting moppers-up.*—A certain number of bombing squads will normally be required with mopping-up parties, their particular duty being to clear communication trenches.

These squads must move with the mopping-up parties; their position in the jumping-off trenches must be selected in such a way as to bring them, when they advance, direct to the entrance of the communication trench allotted to them, so that no time may be lost in getting to work.

Usually it will be sufficient if two or three riflemen are detailed to assist each squad by their fire, but where the communication trench is long, or known to contain dugouts for a large number of men, it may be necessary to detail a Lewis gun and a Stokes mortar to work with the bombers.

5. *Repulsing counterattacks.*—These bombers are required to construct and hold bombing blocks in the communication trenches leading forward from the captured position, the blocks being formed in the general outpost line.

The bombers are required immediately the position is captured, and therefore must be well forward in the assaulting column. Usually they should move with the reserves of the leading companies; they are then available for use in case of a temporary check, and can be thrown in at once by the company commander to work round the flanks of the obstruction.

6. *Gaining touch with flank units.*—Bombers detailed for this duty should advance with and on the outer flanks of the reserve companies. They are then available for use in case of a temporary check. (See par. 5.)

On reaching the objective, they at once start working outward toward the next unit on the flank; riflemen, with a Lewis gun, and a Stokes mortar if it can be got up in time, must be detailed to support them.

7. A bombing attack with the object of gaining ground to the front after the objective has been reached should never be resorted to if it can possibly be avoided.

An advance across the open, under cover of Stokes mortar and flank machine-gun fire, has always a better chance of success, provided the attack has been well organized.

A bombing attack is very slow; it entails great fatigue, not only among the actual bombers but also among the carrying parties who have to keep up the supply of bombs, and the casualties are usually out of all proportion to the gains realized.

Where a bombing attack has to be resorted to, it must always be supported by Lewis guns, Stokes mortars, and riflemen, and the most careful and detailed arrangements made for their co-operation.

8. The difficulty of keeping up an adequate supply of bombs during the fight is another disadvantage of bombing attacks. Wild, indiscriminate throwing produces no results and wastes a large number of bombs; the moral and material effect of a few well-directed salvos, followed up by a determined rush by the bayonet men, is, however, very great.

9. *Rifle grenade.*—More practice in using rifle grenades is required. Every bomber must be trained to use them. The combination of hand and rifle grenades must be made a special feature in all bombing operations.

XXIII. Synchronization of Watches.

The importance of this is not always realized, especially by junior officers.

The effect which even a difference of 30 seconds between watches may have on the chances of success of an assault has already been pointed out. (Sec. III.)

All officers must acquire the habit of checking their watches daily with the official time, which can be obtained from the Signal Service. Commanders must pay special attention to this point during training.

When watches are being synchronized before an attack, the staff or other officers employed on this duty should always carry two watches, as one may get out of order. It is always safer to send a watch round to lower formations—at any rate, once a day—than to rely on sending the correct time by telephone.

XXIV. Carrying Parties and Dumps.

1. The careful organization, and the training in their duties, of carrying parties is of special importance; unless the troops occupying a captured position are amply supplied with munitions, stores, water, and food they will have difficulty in repulsing enemy counterattacks. It is therefore essential that the forward flow of munitions, etc., to the captured position should commence at the earliest possible moment after the assault.

2. The relay system has been found to be the most satisfactory means of working, one group of parties working between the brigade and battalion dumps and a second group between the battalion dump and the captured position. The brigade dumps are filled and replenished under divisional arrangements by means of the tramway, horsed vehicles, or special carrying parties.

All carrying parties should wear a distinctive mark. Otherwise they are liable to be treated as stragglers when returning from the front.

3. *Brigade carrying parties.*—The duty of these parties is to keep the battalion dumps supplied with any stores required.

The brigade bombing officer, working under the staff captain, is usually the best man to supervise these parties, which should normally consist of 1 officer and 20 other ranks for each battalion dump to be maintained.

4. *Battalion carrying parties.*—(*a*) There are various ways of organizing these parties, but it seems preferable for each company to detail two sections, or a platoon if necessary, to carry for it. These parties will have to make two or three journeys to get up all the stores required. As this entails passing backward and forward through the hostile barrage, a determined N.C.O. must be put in command of each party.

(*b*) The trench dump will be emptied first, after which stores will be drawn direct from the battalion dump. The stores to be sent up in each journey should be worked out and arranged accordingly in the dumps.

An officer or specially selected N.C.O. must be detailed to supervise the work of these carrying parties.

(*c*) The order of importance in which the stores are required in the captured position is as follows:

(1) *Grenades, hand and rifle.*—Each man detailed to carry grenades must carry two boxes. Grenades should not be carried

in sandbags, sacks, or carriers, as they are liable to get mislaid or overlooked.

All grenades must have the detonators inserted before leaving the brigade dump.

(2) *Picks and shovels.*—A certain quantity, in addition to those taken up by the consolidating party, must be sent up for the use of the leading waves. They should be made up in bundles of five shovels or four picks. For ordinary soil one pick to every two shovels is required.

(3) S. A. A. This will depend on the amount carried by each man of the assaulting companies. Probably five boxes per assaulting company will be sufficient to start with.

(4) *Sandbags.*—Each man of the carrying party should carry 10 in addition to his other load.

(5) *Water.*—The 2-gallon petrol tins previously stored near the front line should be carried up. One man can not carry more than one tin over bad ground and when under shell fire.

(6) S. O. S. rockets, Very's light cartridges and flares for communicating with contact aeroplanes.

(7) Wiring material.

(8) Rations.

The stores for the first journey must be taken forward in the last wave of the assaulting columns.

5. *Formations.*—Carrying parties should move in small columns in single file; they are easier to control in this formation than when in extended order.

The commander of each party must follow in rear of his party; otherwise half the loads will never reach their destination.

6. *Salvage.*—Carrying parties should not be allowed to come back empty handed from the front line. They can be used as escort to prisoners or to assist in carrying down wounded. If not required for these duties, each man should bring back a rifle and equipment taken from the dead or badly wounded.

7. *Stokes mortar ammunition.*—It will probably be found advisable to detail a special carrying party to work right through from the brigade dump to the mortars in action. This party should work under the orders of the battery commander.

Four rounds in sandbags make a load for one man.

8. *Issue of stores.*—The stores which have been specially arranged for, vide 4 (*b*), will be sent up automatically from battalion and trench dumps. No other stores will be issued without a written demand signed by an officer. Similarly no stores will be issued from brigade dumps without such a signature.

9. *Organization of dumps in the captured position.*—Company commanders must pay special attention to forming dumps in the captured position. S.A.A., bombs, flares, and iron rations should be collected from casualties lying in the vicinity of the trench.

All serviceable enemy rifles, S.A.A., machine guns, bombs, tools, sandbags, wire, revetting material, and rations should be collected and used up first, in order to husband our own munitions, etc., and thereby reduce the work of carrying parties.

XXV. RATIONS AND WATER.

An assault, followed by hard digging in consolidation, entails great physical exertion on the part of all ranks engaged in it. Therefore they require an ample supply of food and water, if their physical energy is to be maintained.

Every possible effort must be made to get rations, including rum and water forward to the captured position as soon as possible; this is not difficult where the subject has been carefully thought out and preliminary arrangements made before the assault. It is useless waiting till the assault has been made before commencing preparations; unless arrangements have been made beforehand it will generally be impossible to get rations forward the first night.

Practice is required during training, and although it is impossible to reproduce the actual conditions of bad ground, shell and rifle fire, all ranks concerned can learn a good deal from one or two practices carried out after dark.

The first night after the assault is the most important and the most difficult to deal with.

After a heavy bombardment and the subsequent enemy barrage the ground will be badly cut up; there will not have been time to open up the roads and to fill in or bridge the enemy trenches; consequently it will seldom be possible to use wheeled transport.

Pack animals will have to be used to carry rations to battalion headquarters, at least, and possibly further, to lighten the work of the carrying parties. All pack animals in the division should be pooled for this purpose and should be assembled as far forward as possible during the afternoon; wheeled transports should bring the rations, etc., up to this point, and all loads must be transferred *before dark*.

Transport officers of the units engaged must go forward and reconnoiter the route to their units during daylight; they must not rely entirely on guides, although the latter must be used as well.

The convoys must be sent off *immediately* after dark; bad ground, hostile shelling, and darkness all tend to make progress very slow; a late start involves the risk of not being able to finish the task before daylight.

An officer of the Q.M.G. branch of the divisional staff must be detailed to supervise all the arrangements; this officer must make it his business to see that the rations, etc., do actually reach the troops concerned and that they are not dumped anywhere along the route.

For carrying up water on pack animals, a wooden crate to hold two 2-gallon petrol tins has been found useful, two crates forming a load.

The supply of sufficient 2-gallon petrol tins is limited; all empty tins must be collected and sent back with the ration convoys. They must not be left lying about in the trenches.

XXVI. PRISONERS.

Surrenders.—It is the duty of all ranks to continue to use their weapons against the enemy's fighting troops, unless and until it is beyond all doubt that these have not only ceased all resistance, but that, whether through having voluntarily thrown down their weapons or otherwise, they have definitely and finally abandoned all hope or intention of resisting further. In the case of apparent surrender, it lies with the enemy to prove his intention beyond the possibility of misunderstanding before the surrender can be accepted as genuine.

Size of escorts.—These should not exceed 10 per cent of the prisoners in each batch; no more men than are absolutely necessary should be sent back from the front line; carrying parties returning for more stores and slightly wounded walking cases should be used where possible.

XXVII. WOUNDED.

Slight wounds.—Officers and men who are wounded in the course of the operations, but whose wounds do not wholly incapacitate them, should continue to take an active part in the fight until ordered to the rear by a superior officer.

The presence of a wounded officer, N.C.O., or man in the ranks, who, though wounded, has the grit to continue fighting, is a fine example of courage and·most.inspiring to his comrades.

Discarding of arms and equipment.—Wounded men must not be allowed to discard their arms and equipment unless their wounds are so severe as to render the men incapable of carrying them.

The soldier must be taught that it is a point of honor to carry his arms as long as he possibly can. Lightly wounded walking cases, who have disobeyed this order, should be sent back by the trench police to fetch their rifles and equipment.

XXVIII. ENEMY RUSES.

Words of command.—(*a*) It must be impressed on all officers and men that the command " Retire " does not exist. It is, however, frequently used by the enemy in the hope of misleading our troops and causing them to fall back. Any individual giving this command must be treated as an enemy.

(*b*) It is only in exceptional circumstances that troops should be ordered to withdraw. In such cases the order must emanate from an officer, the word "withdraw" must be used, and a definite point or line on to which the withdrawal is to be conducted must be given. Further, the name of the officer giving the order must be indicated.

Stretcher bearers.—The enemy carry their machine guns on a sledge and sometimes throw a blanket over the gun. At a distance this makes the sledge and gun resemble a stretcher. Enemy stretcher bearers should therefore be treated with suspicion.

XXIX. RELIEFS.

Relief of troops who have captured a position should be carried out over the open as far as possible; there is then less chance of confusion or of troops losing their way than when the relief is carried out through strange, and probably damaged, communication trenches.

A good deal of relief can often be completed in daylight, if it is carried out by dribbling forward small parties; there is usually considerable movement going on behind the line, carrying parties, stretcher bearers, etc., so that small parties will often escape notice.

Overland routes should be marked out with tape or rope and pickets; this is especially required at night.

Particular care must be taken.to see that the outpost line is taken over correctly; as a rule outgoing units should leave their machine guns, Lewis guns, snipers, and scouts in the line for 24 hours after relief in order that the incoming unit may be able to establish itself properly.

XXX. Number of Officers, etc., to Take Part in the Assault.

1. Infantry battalions, machine gun companies, and Stokes mortar batteries must not go into an attack with their full complement of officers, N.C.O.'s, riflemen, gunners, and specialists; a certain proportion must be left behind in order to provide a nucleus on which to reorganize the battalion in the event of heavy casualties.

2. The following are the minimum number which must be left behind on each occasion when the battalion takes part in au attack:

(*a*) *Officers.*—(1) *Battalion headquarters.*—Either the C.O. or the second in command.

(2) *Each company.*—Either the company commander or the second in command. Not more than two company commanders are to go in with their companies. Not more than 20 officers, excluding the medical officer, are to go in with the battalion.

(*b*) *N.C.O.'s and riflemen.*—(1) Two company sergeants major.

(2) *Each company.*—One sergeant, 1 corporal, and 1 lance corporal.

(3) *Each platoon.*—Three privates.

(*c*) *Specialists*, that is, Lewis gunners, scouts, snipers, signalers, and runners, 33 per cent of each category; in the case of Lewis gunners, only 2 gunners are to be sent forward with each gun. (Sec. XVII, par. 5.)

3. In the case of machine-gun companies and Stokes mortar batteries a minimum of 25 per cent of officers, sergeants, corporals, and gunners must be left behind by each unit.

4. The officers and other ranks left behind should normally remain at their transport lines until their unit comes out of the line.

In the event of a unit which has sustained heavy casualties in leaders and specialists being required to remain in the front line for some days after the assault, the brigade commander will order forward such officers and other ranks as he may consider necessary to maintain the unit in an efficient condition.

XXXI. Dress and Equipment.

1. *Officers.*—All infantry officers, taking part in an attack, must be dressed and equipped exactly the same as their men. Sticks are not to be carried.

2. *Fighting dress.*—The following is suggested as the normal fighting dress for all ranks of Infantry, machine gun, Stokes mortar, and Engineer units:

(*a*) *Clothing, etc., worn on the men.*—As issued.

(*b*) *Arms.*—As issued.

(*c*) *Intrenching tool.*—As issued.

(*d*) *Accouterments.*—As issued, with the exception of the pack. The haversack will be carried on the back in place of the pack.

(*e*) Box respirator and tube helmet.

(*f*) *Articles carried in the haversack.*—Cap comforter, cardigan jacket when issued, towel and soap, spare oil tin, holdall, iron ration, waterproof sheet; the latter will be carried on top of the haversack under the flap.

The mess tin and cover will be slung outside the haversack.

In cold weather the greatcoat will be carried instead of the waterproof sheet; it will be rolled and attached to the waist-belt underneath the haversack.

(*g*) *Ammunition.*—170 rounds, except for bombers, signalers, scouts, runners, machine, Lewis and Stokes mortar gunners, and carrying parties, who will carry only 50 rounds.

(*h*) *No. 5 Mills hand grenades.*—Two, carried one in each top pocket of the jacket. These grenades are intended to be collected into a dump as soon as the objective has been gained, and are not to be used by the individual except in an emergency.

(*i*) *Aeroplane flares.*—Two, carried one in each bottom pocket of the jacket. These are intended to be collected into a dump as soon as the objective has been gained, and then to be issued as required. They are not required by engineer, pioneer, machine gun, and Stokes mortar units.

(*j*) *Sandbags.*—Three, carried under the braces across the back.

(*k*) *Rations and water.*—One iron ration in haversack.

Unexpended portion of current day's ration and one tin solidified alcohol in mess tin.

One filled water bottle. Men must be trained to drink sparingly.

3. *Disposal of surplus clothing and equipment.*—The surplus clothing and equipment of each man will be tied up in the pack, which will be stored under cover at the unit's transport lines or in some suitable building if available.

4. In addition to the munitions and stores mentioned in paragraph 2, the following stores, etc., will be carried by special parties:

(*a*) *S.A.A.*—One bandolier (50 rounds) by the consolidating parties of the assaulting companies and by all N.C.O.'s and men, except specialists, of the reserve companies. This ammunition will be collected into a dump when the men reach their objective.

(*b*) *Wire cutters and breakers.*—Wire cutters and breakers should be carried by the two leading waves of the assaulting companies and by the leading men of the reserve companies, those available for the battalion being distributed in the proportion of two to assaulting companies to one to reserve companies.

When a brigade has more than one objective, the brigade commander must give a larger proportion to the battalions detailed for the further objective, as the wire may not be so well cut as in the case of the first objective.

Wire cutters must be attached to the man's shoulder strap by a string, and the cutters tucked into his waistbelt.

(*c*) *Picks and shovels.*—Every man of the consolidating party of assaulting companies, and 50 per cent of the reserve companies, must carry one pick or one shovel.

The tools should be carried on the back under the haversack with the head of the tool resting on the top of the haversack.

(*d*) *S.O.S. rockets.*—Twelve should be carried by each company, to be distributed among the reserve.

(*e*) *Artillery flags or disks.*—One to be carried by a selected N.C.O. or man in each platoon of assaulting units.

(*f*) *P. grenades.*—Carried by mopping-up parties.

(*g*) *Hand and rifle grenades.*—Carried by bombers either in waistcoats, haversacks, or canvas buckets. Not more than 15 grenades per man. Every man must carry a supply of at least 5 rods and 5 blank cartridges for use with the rifle grenade.

Very's pistols should not be taken forward with assaulting troops, owing to the risk of casualties and of the pistols being thereby lost; they should be kept back at battalion headquarters and sent up after the objective has been gained.

5. *Issue of S.A.A., tools, etc.*—In order to save the men unnecessary fatigue, the S.A.A., grenades, tools, flares, S.O.S. rockets, etc., mentioned in paragraphs 2 and 4, which are not part of the man's ordinary equipment, should be issued at a forward dump just before the men enter the trenches; probably a brigade dump will be found convenient.

These stores, which are additional to the establishment fixed for the dump, should be laid out beforehand, so that no time may be lost in issuing them.

XXXII. Distinguishing Marks.

1. Distinguishing marks to denote different battalions or companies will be worn on the arms immediately below the point of the shoulder.

2. In addition, specialists and carrying parties of infantry units will wear distinguishing marks as follows:

Scouts_____Green band.
Runners_____Red band.
Regimental and company signalers_ Blue band.
Carrying parties_____Yellow band.
Mopping-up parties_____ White band.
Salvage parties_____Khaki band, with
        " Salvage " in
        red letters.

These bands will be $1\frac{1}{2}$ inches wide, made from material obtained locally, and will be worn round the left forearm.

3. Men equipped with wire cutters or wire breakers will wear a piece of white tape tied to the right shoulder strap.

XXXIII. Documents and Maps.

All ranks taking part in an assault are forbidden to carry any letters, papers, orders, or sketches which, in the event of their capture, would be likely to give any information to the enemy.

Officers should not be overburdened with maps; the trench map of the actual area and possibly the local 1/100,000 sheet are all they require for the assault.

Appendix A.

---

1. *Reconnaissance.*—(*a*) The corps allots the task to be executed by the division. The divisional commander will be informed of the frontage, objectives, and assembly area allotted to his division, as well as the Artillery support he may expect and the action of the divisions on his flank.

(*b*) Before the divisional commander can formulate his plans of attack, reconnaissance on the following points is necessary:

(1) The ground over which the attack is to take place.

(2) The enemy's system of trenches, namely, his front trenches, support trenches, machine-gun emplacements, communication trenches, rear lines, strong points, and wire.

(3) The area and trenches in which his own troops will assemble.

(*c*) A good deal of the above information can be obtained from study of aeroplane photographs, but personal observation by the divisional commander and his staff is also needed.

(*d*) Information gained thus must constantly be added to from information obtained by patrolling and observation.

(*e*) Similarly brigade and battalion commanders, as soon as they have been allotted their tasks, must reconnoiter before they can prepare their plans.

(*f*) Reconnaissance by commanders, staff, and regimental officers, including M.G. officers, and a proportion of N.C.O.'s, signalers, and runners, of reserve divisions is quite as important as for officers and other ranks of front-line divisions.

Not only must they be familiar with every detail of the enemy's lines but they must also have a thorough knowledge of our own trench system, so that when orders are received for the reserve division to move forward no time may be lost in reconnoitering lines of advance to our own front line.

2. *Artillery preparation.*—(*a*) The Artillery preparation now certain extent outside the province of the divisional

commander, as the Artillery plan, except for minor operations, will be coordinated by the corps Artillery commander, under the orders of the corps commander, after consultation with the divisional commanders concerned.

(*b*) It is, however, the duty of the divisional commander to make himself thoroughly acquainted with the Artillery plan, so far as it affects his task, and to bring to the notice of the corps commander any points which he considers require more preparation, or any modifications in the plan which he may think necessary to insure the successful completion of his task.

(*c*) Commanders of lower formations—i. e., brigades and battalions—must go through the Artillery plan, so far as it affects them, and study it on the ground with the commander of the Artillery detailed to support them, in order to insure that they are in agreement as to how the plan is to be carried out.

3. *Organization of trenches for the attack.*—This includes—

(*a*) Advancing front trenches to within assaulting distance.

(*b*) Preparation of forming-up places (assembly trenches).

(*c*) Digging of communication trenches.

(*d*) Sapping forward for communication trenches.

(*e*) Putting up direction boards.

(*f*) Preparation of exits from trenches.

(*g*) Preparation of routes for reserves.

(*a*) The front-line or jumping-off trench *must be not more than 200 yards from* the enemy's front line, and as nearly parallel as possible to that line, to insure that the leading waves jump off square to their objective.

(*b*) The work required under this heading depends on the plan and the formations to be adopted.

The general principles are as follows:

The leading two or three waves will consist of men in extended order, therefore continuous trenches parallel to the front jumping-off trench are necessary.

Not more than two waves can be accommodated in one trench.

The subsequent waves will move in line or in section columns; short T's or sidings off communication trenches form the quickest method of obtaining the accommodation required.

The system of assembly trenches must conform as far as possible to the existing trench system in order to obtain concealment.

Reserves can usually be accommodated in the reserve lines of the front-line system and in the intermediate system without much additional labor.

(c) The ideal to aim at is as follows:

On each brigade front of attack, to within 800 yards of the front line, one " IN " and one " OUT " trench.

On each battalion front of attack, within 800 yards of the front line, one " IN " and one " OUT " trench.

On each company front of attack, one " IN " and one " OUT " trench for the depth of the company zone of assembly.

Trenches allotted as " OUT " trenches, unless specially dug for the purpose, must have the corners of the traverses or zigzags rounded off to allow of the passage of stretchers.

If desired, special trenches can be allotted for wounded only.

A map showing " IN " and " OUT " traffic in communication trenches must be prepared and issued down to company commanders, trenches available for stretchers being specially marked.

This map need not be accurately drawn to scale; a diagrammatic sketch with distances marked on it is sufficient.

All traffic in communication trenches must be regulated, and regimental police must be told off for this duty.

Where time does not permit of digging the necessary communication trenches, some trenches will have to be used for both " IN " and " OUT " traffic; in this case they must be provided with passing places, formed either by widening the trench or by digging short sidings long enough to take a stretcher; such sidings are required every 25 yards. Extra police must also be detailed for such a trench.

(d) Russian saps must be run out as far as possible across " No Man's Land," to be opened up immediately after the assault as communication trenches or for use previous to the assault for installing boring machines, trench mortars, machine guns, or flame projectors. One sap, if provided with a number of offshoots, can be used for all five purposes.

As these saps will normally be constructed by tunneling companies, the work will be coordinated by the corps; but this will not relieve the divisional commander of the responsibility of making preparations for opening up communication trenches across " No Man's Land " by running out saps.

(e) Trenches must be clearly labeled with plainly marked signboards.

" In " and " out " trenches, in addition to their names, must be marked with special boards: Black letters on a white ground for " in " trenches, white letters on a black ground for " out " trenches. All lettering to be 6 inches high and each board to have a directing arrow.

(*f*) For the leading waves, which move in line and must therefore leave the trenches simultaneously, ladders or steps are necessary.

If ladders are used, all those used in one bay should be fixed together top and bottom by planks to prevent a ladder falling. Care must be taken that the tops of ladders do not project over the parapet.

Stakes 3 to 4 feet long driven into the parapet to act as handles when climbing ladders are useful.

For the subsequent waves, when moving in column, short zigzag saps, run out from the trench and terminating in a ramp, form the most convenient exit.

Provision must be made for bridges over the front line trenches for the rear waves.

(*g*) Overland routes for reserves moving up to the front line must be reconnoitered and marked out. Plenty of direction boards with arrows are required, and these boards must be erected so as to be inconspicuous to the enemy. All trenches crossing the route must be bridged, bridges to be wide enough to take men in file.

4. *Observation posts.*—These are required for divisional and brigade commanders and staffs.

They must be provided with adequate accommodation and bombproof cover.

It will sometimes be necessary to use artillery O.P.'s to obtain the best view and to economize communications.

In addition O.P.'s are required for brigade observers, who should be posted where they can watch the advance and report its progress. Telephone communication to brigade headquarters is essential.

5. *Command posts.*—Shell-proof command posts (battle headquarters) for divisional and brigade headquarters, and possibly for battalion headquarters, will be required, though in the latter case, if the existing battalion headquarters are unsuitable, it will usually suffice to convert one of the forward company headquarters into battalion headquarters.

Artillery command posts in close proximity to those of the division and the brigades will be required for the officers commanding the artillery supporting the division and the brigades, respectively.

The requisites of a good command post are:

(*a*) It must be proof against 8-inch shells.

(*b*) Covered ingress and egress must be provided.

(*c*) A good O.P. should be available close by with a covered approach thereto.

(*d*) Sufficient accommodation must be provided for orderlies.

In the case of division and brigade headquarters, the command posts should be reasonably near a road in order to simplify the task of dispatch riders.

As the positions of these command posts effect the system of signal communications to a great extent, they must be settled at the earliest possible moment to allow of the communication scheme being arranged.

6. *Signal service.*—(*a*) The establishment of the signal system, i. e., telegraph and telephone, will be coordinated as a whole by the corps.

The divisional commander must make himself acquainted with the scheme and satisfy himself that it meets with his requirements.

The principal points which require attention are:

(1) Cable communication, buried 6 feet deep, must exist between the divisional command post and the front trenches.

(2) All Artillery and Infantry command posts and observation posts in the area between the divisional command post and the front trenches must be linked up with the buried system. Command posts on the flanks of the area must also be linked up with the buried systems of formations on the flanks.

(3) All wires in communication trenches must be securely fastened and must not be allowed to interfere with traffic in any way.

(4) Where time is short, commence burying cable at the front-line trench and work backwards.

The provision of bomb-proof accommodation for telephone exchanges is essential. If labor is scarce, telephone exchanges must be completed before the cable is buried.

(*b*) The visual signaling scheme must be worked out and sites for stations both in our own and in the enemy's lines selected.

When prepared, the scheme should be issued, in the form of a diagram, down to battalion and battery commanders.

If time permits, good value will be obtained by making receiving and transmitting stations within our own lines shell proof.

7. *Employment of R.E. and pioneers.*—The general policy for the employment of R.E. and pioneers will be laid down by the corps, but the divisional engineer and pioneer units will be required to undertake some or all of the following works in the divisional zone:

(*a*) Construction of observation stations for commanders and staffs.

(*b*) Construction of command posts.

(*c*) Construction of communication trenches (supervision of Infantry working parties).

(*d*) Sapping forward into "No Man's Land" where Russian saps are nonexistent.

(*e*) Construction and fixing of bridges for crossing our own trenches and disused trenches in "No Man's Land."

(*f*) Construction and fixing of ladders and making ramps to provide exits from our trenches.

(*g*) Water supply.

(*h*) Formation of R.E. depots.

(*i*) Construction of aid posts and dressing stations. Supervision only; labor must be provided by medical units.

(*j*) Construction of additional tramways and provision of ample rolling stock.

(*k*) Clearing and repairing roads up to the front line and bridging trenches crossing the roads for passage of Artillery and M.T.

(*l*) Provision of bridges for crossing enemy's front-line trenches to allow Artillery to move forward.

(*m*) Provision of signboards for captured trenches.

The Infantry must dig their own assembly and forming-up trenches, and must clear the necessary passages through our own wire.

As regards (*g*), the water-supply scheme for the corps area, including arrangements for extending the system to the captured trenches, will probably be worked out by the corps, but an endeavor must be made to get the water laid on in pipes as near as possible to the front trenches.

In addition, arrangements must be made for storing water in tanks or barrels in or near the front-line trenches, and also at battalion and brigade headquarters.

As regards (*h*), this is dealt with under paragraph 8.

8. *Formation of store depots or dumps.*—(*a*) The following dumps will normally be required:

> A main divisional dump.
> An advanced divisional dump.
> One or more brigade dumps.
> Battalion dumps.
> Trench dumps.

(*b*) The *main divisional dump* should be established at the tramway terminus.

The *advanced divisional dump* should be regarded as an emergency dump to be drawn from only when the tramway breaks down. It should be established well forward on the tramway system, preferably at the point where the tram lines branch off to the brigade dumps, and also, if possible, near a road to enable it to be filled from wagons.

The *brigade dumps*, one for each brigade in front line, should be established in the vicinity of brigade battle headquarters, or, if the tramway system extends beyond this point, then at the tramway railhead.

The *battalion dumps*, one for each battalion in front line, should be established close to battalion headquarters.

The *trench dumps* should be established in the front line and support trenches just off " IN " communication trenches.

(*c*) In establishing these dumps the principle must be to scatter the stores allotted to each dump in a number of small subdumps, sufficiently far apart to prevent one shell exploding more than one subdump; on the other hand, the subdumps must not be so scattered that an unnecessary number of storekeepers is required.

Each of the subdumps should contain a proportion of the ammunition, grenades, rockets, etc., allotted to the dump.

All perishable stores in dumps, except those in main divisional dump, must, if possible, be in bomb-proof dugouts.

(*d*) All dumps should contain the following stores:

> S.A.A.
> Grenades, hand and rifle.
> Very's lights.
> S.O.S. rockets.
> Aeroplane flares.

In addition, dumps should contain special stores, as follows:

Main divisional dump.—Stokes mortar ammunition, trench mortar ammunition, P. grenades. R.E. stores (i. e., picks, shovels, sandbags, wire cutters, tracing tape, timber).

Advanced divisional dump.—As for main divisional dump, omitting wire cutters and timber.

Brigade dump.—Stokes mortar ammunition, trench mortar ammunition, P. grenades, R.E. stores (i. e., picks, shovels, sandbags, tracing tape, wire, and screw pickets); 5,000[1] bully beef, biscuit, and rum rations; 200[1] petrol tins filled with water.

Battalion dump.—R.E. stores (i. e., picks, shovels, sandbags, wire, and screw pickets), 100 petrol tins filled with water.

No special R.E. stores are required in the *trench dumps*, but the tools and stores already in the trenches for maintenance purposes should be collected into these dumps.

(*e*) A specially selected officer should be in charge of the divisional dumps and should be made responsible for keeping brigade dumps supplied.

The brigade bombing officer should be in charge of the brigade dump and should be made responsible for keeping battalion dumps supplied.

An officer or specially selected N.C.O., under the adjutant, should be in charge of the battalion dump and be responsible for sending forward stores to fighting troops as required.

A small permanent loading and unloading party is required at the divisional and brigade dumps.

An officer, with traffic staff, is required for working the tramways, and he allots truck accommodation on demand of officers in charge of dumps.

Each dump, except trench dumps, requires a storekeeper.

9. *Police arrangements and traffic control.*—The control of traffic in rear of the trench system will normally be undertaken by the corps.

Divisions will have to make arrangements for the following through their A.P.M.'s.—(*a*) Policing of main communication trenches up to brigade battle headquarters. Forward of this point brigades will be responsible. "IN" and "OUT" routes must be strictly adhered to by all ranks, the only exceptions being staff officers, signal personnel, and Artillery linemen repairing lines, runners and trench maintenance gangs, who may be

---

[1] Reserve supplies for troops in forward area.

permitted to use any trench required for the execution of their duty.

(*b*) *Establishing stragglers' posts.*—These are normally established at the exits of main " OUT " communication trenches.

All unwounded men will be collected there, formed into organized bodies and sent back to their units.

It is usually advisable to establish these posts in the vicinity of dressing stations, so that unarmed and unequipped stragglers can be reequipped and rearmed from the arms and equipment taken from casualties at the dressing station.

If possible, arrangements should be made for giving the men tea, bully beef, and biscuit before sending them up to the trenches again.

(*c*) *Evacuation of prisoners.*—Fighting troops will escort prisoners back as far as brigade battle headquarters. From there they must be collected under divisional arrangements and escorted to corps cages.

10. *Medical arrangements.*—As a rule, the corps will arrange all details up to and including the main dressing stations.

The A.D.M.S. will, under the orders of the divisional commander, be responsible for the following:

(*a*) Provision of advanced dressing stations. These must be shellproof and as near as possible to roads fit for motor ambulances.

(*b*) Provision of regimental aid posts in shellproof dugouts.

(*c*) Arrangements for evacuating to A.D.S. by tramway.

(*d*) Selection of and marking of routes for walking cases, including collecting stations.

(*e*) Allotment of traffic routes to ambulance vehicles within the forward area.

(*f*) Plans for cooperation of field ambulance bearers and regimental stretcher bearers.

Any work required under these headings must be executed by field ambulance personnel, any technical assistance required being given by the C.R.E.

APPENDIX B.

INSTRUCTIONS FOR CONTACT PATROL WORK BY AEROPLANES.

1. *Object.*—Contact patrol work by aeroplane is designed—

(*a*) To keep headquarters of formations informed as to the progress of their troops during an attack.

(*b*) To report on the positions of the enemy opposing the advance, the movement of his immediate reserves, and the state of his defenses.

(*c*) To transmit messages from the troops engaged to the headquarters of their formation.

Contact patrols supplement but in no way take the place of other systems of communication.

Observers must be fully informed as to the plan of attack, the disposition of the troops with whom they are working, and their objectives. Before going up, the observer should always, if possible, visit the division or, if the operation is a small one, the brigade concerned, in order to obtain all the detailed information possible. He should synchronize his watch with the staff. so that he may know exactly when to look for the attack to commence. As much notice as possible should be given to the squadron concerned when a contact patrol is required, in order that the observer may have time to make these visits.

2. *Recognition of aeroplane.*—Aeroplanes detailed for contact patrol work must have special markings, which should be known to all ranks of the Infantry with which they are working. They will, in addition, carry a Klaxon horn and Very's lights for the purpose of making themselves known, and to answer signals received from the ground. Infantry may, as a general rule, expect to see their contact patrol machine vertically above our own and the enemy's trenches.

3. *Information sent to our Artillery.*—Aeroplanes on contact patrol must not be called upon to report regarding hostile batteries (but see par. 7), or to check the fire of our Artillery, which is the duty of the machines working with the Artillery. From the position from which they work they are, however, very well

placed to keep our Artillery informed as to the movements of the enemy in immediate contact with our Infantry (see par. 7.)

4. *Methods of communication between Infantry and aeroplanes.*—Contact patrol aeroplanes receive signals from—

(A) Attacking Infantry; (B) battalion and brigade headquarters.

(A) Attacking Infantry signal to the aeroplane by means of flares. Flares will be lit:

(*a*) By previous arrangement, (1) at specified times, (2) at specified places.

. The former is, as a rule, the preferable plan.

The approximate hours at which flares will be lit should be laid down in orders. At these hours the Infantry will be on the lookout and will light their flares when their aeroplane calls for them by Klaxon horn. (See par. 5.) About half an hour after the objective is expected to be reached has been found a suitable time.

(*b*) Without previous arrangement, (1) when called for by the aeroplane by Klaxon horn (see par. 5); (2) on the initiative of local commanders who may wish to make their position known.

Flares should only be lit by the order of local commanders when the aeroplane working with their formation is flying in their vicinity.

When flares are called for by the aeroplane, it is important that they should be lit by the most advanced troops. Bodies of troops in rear will often light flares, thinking that they are the most advanced, but this will not prevent the location of the front line, provided flares are also lit there.

Flares can be seen, if lit, at the bottom of trenches or in shell holes, but care must be taken that there is no obstruction between the flare and the aeroplane. At least two flares per man should be carried by troops in the attack. The signal by Klaxon horn to call for flares will be a succession of A.'s. (See par. 5.) If the Infantry can not reply at once, they should await a repetition of the signal before lighting their flares; otherwise they may be lit when the observer is not in a position to see them.

(B) (1) Battalion and brigade headquarters indicate their position and identity to the aeroplane by means of ground signal sheets and strips. Ground signal sheets (see Table I) are laid on the ground at the headquarters concerned to indicate its position, while its identity is disclosed by the code letters of the battalion or brigade, made by ground signal strips, laid alongside the sheet, or sent on the panel or lamp (see (2) below), if strips are not available. Sheets and strips must be put out as soon as the headquarters is established and left out until it moves.

(2) Battalion and brigade headquarters send messages to the aeroplane by means of (a) ground signal panel; (b) lamp.

Ground signal strips will not be used for the purpose.

Complicated systems of communication are bound to break down in battle, and signals sent by the above means will therefore be confined to those given in Table I.

Headquarters will indicate that they have a message for the aeroplane by displaying the white side of their ground signal panel or by shining their lamp on the aeroplane. When the aeroplane is ready to receive a message, it will send the code letters of the headquarters concerned, followed by the letter G, by Klaxon or lamp, using the Morse code.

Each word or code letter of a message from the ground will be answered by the aeroplane by the general answer T, and the receipt of the message will be acknowledged by the code letters of the sender, followed by R.D. (See par. 5.)

Ground signal sheets, strips, or panels must be carefully sited in order to give the aeroplane observer a dark background if possible.

In signaling to an aeroplane from the ground, it is essential that—

(a) Signalers should know when the aeroplane is in a position to receive and when it is not.

(b) Signaling should be slow, and particular attention should be paid to timing and to the correct formation of letters.

(c) Signalers on the ground should have patience, and continue sending until their signals are acknowledged.

5. *Methods of communication between aeroplane and Infantry.*—Contact patrol aeroplanes communicate with the attacking Infantry by means of Klaxon horns, using one signal only, namely, a succession of A.'s, meaning "light flares." If the Klaxon fails to act, or if no reply is received, the aeroplane will fire a white light, indicating a call for flares. They communicate with headquarters of battalions and brigades by means of (a) Klaxon horns; (b) lamps, using the Morse code in both cases.

6. *Methods of communication between aeroplanes and headquarters of corps and divisions.*—Aeroplanes communicate with the headquarters of corps and divisions by dropping message bags.

Observers should be provided with tracings on a suitable scale and showing all known trenches, on which the positions reached by our own troops will be marked as follows:

Flares   =   ------

Battalion H.Q. =   🌓   with battalion call letters.

Brigade H.Q. =   🌓   with brigade call letters.

When necessary, the tracing should be supplemented by a message.

On reaching the ground the observer will report personally or by telephone to the headquarters concerned.

7. *Method of communication between contact patrol aeroplanes and the Artillery.*—Wireless will only be used by contact patrol aeroplanes for the purpose of sending down targets to our Artillery. Such targets will be sent down under the zone-call system as used by Artillery machines. Contact patrol machines should watch especially for movements of immediate reserves, massing of troops for counterattack, minenwerfers, machine guns, and strong points holding up our advance, and targets of such nature. Hostile batteries will normally be dealt with by the Artillery machines.

8. *Special reconnaissances.*—In addition to establishing communication between the Infantry and the headquarters of formations, contact patrol aeroplanes may be employed to report on the enemy's dispositions and defenses both before and during an attack.

Prior to an attack they are able to keep the command constantly informed as to the progress and results of the Artillery bombardment, while after an attack they can discover the enemy's fresh dispositions and sometimes his strength at various points. In this case also observers must be given all available information by the staff concerned before starting.

Commanders and staffs, when giving orders for such reconnaissance, must fully consider the risks run by pilots and observers in carrying them out. At an altitude of 1,500 feet or less an aeroplane is almost certain to be hit by rifle and machine-
    ~om the ground, unless the enemy is fully occupied in

fighting. Conditions will arise in which these dangers should and must be run, but it must be borne in mind that the loss of one or two good pilots or observers who know their ground impairs the value and efficiency of squadrons for a considerable time, and is only justified by the chance of obtaining information of really first-class importance. When giving orders the degree of importance attached by the commander to the information required should be explained to observers, who will then be able to judge to some extent the risks which they are justified in incurring. A rough guide as to the height from which various objects can be observed in an average light is given in Table II.

TABLE I.—*Signals between aeroplanes and Infantry.*

1. By the aeroplane: Succession of A.'s on Klaxon horn, followed by white Very's light if necessary.—light flares.

2. By battalion H.Q.: Semicircular ground signal sheet with letters of battalion call, e. g., AL—battalion H.Q.

By brigade H.Q.: Three-quarters circle ground-signal sheet with letters of brigade call, e. g., PN—brigade H.Q.

3. By brigade or battalion H.Q.:

By lamp or signaling panel.	Meaning.	Answer by aeroplanes, by lamp, or klaxon.	Meaning.
Battn. or Bde. call	H. Q. are here	T.	Received.
Succession of I's	Enemy are retiring at	T.	Do.
F's	Enemy offering strong resistance at.	T.	Do.
G's	Further bombardment required.	T.	Do.
H's	Lengthen range	T.	Do.
J's	Raise barrage	T.	Do.
K's	Lower barrage	T.	Do.
O's	Barrage wanted	T.	Do.
P's	Reinforcements wanted	T.	Do.
N's	Short of ammunition	T.	Do.
W's	Short of water	T.	Do.
Y's	Short of grenades	T.	Do.
X's	Held up by M.G. fire	T.	Do.
Z's	Held up by wire	T.	Do.
O. K.	We are all right	T.	Do.

Signals will be preceded by battalion or brigade call letter. if strips have not been put out. The map location of the point of the line to which reference is made will be given, if necessary, by the clock code, the position of the sender being considered as the center of the clock face, hnd the hour 12 being always taken as pointing due north. The distance in yards from the point it is desired to describe will be given by a letter of the alphabet, A, representing 50 yards; B, 100 yards; C, 200; D, 300; and so on. The direction will be given by the hour on the imaginary clock face.

E. g., if it were necessary to ask for the range to be lengthened at a point 400 yards northwest of battalion headquarters, the message would be HHH E 10, HHH being acknowledged by T, and the whole message by the code letters of the sender followed by R.D.

Distances of 150, 250 yards, etc., will be given by a two-letter signal, e. g., BA=150, CA=250.

TABLE II.—*Heights from which various objects can be seen in a good light.*

From 3,000 feet—
> An attack can be followed.
> Bombing can be seen.
> State of trenches can be reported upon, as to whether they have been badly damaged by bombardment or not.
> Trench mortar emplacements can sometimes be seen.
> Tracks can be seen.

From 2,500 feet—
> Men massed in trenches can be seen.
> It can sometimes be seen whether a trench is revetted or not.

From 2,000 feet the following can be seen:
> Wire in a good light (but not its condition).
> Overhead traverses.
> Sandbags.
> Comparative width of trench.

From 1,500 feet the following can be seen:
> Dug-out entrances.
> Comparative depth of trench.
> Men making signals, such as waving their helmets.

From 1,000 feet or under our own troops can be distinguished from those of the enemy.

REMARKS ABOUT THE DETERMINATION OF THE HOUR OF THE ASSAULT.
(CHIEFLY FOR A LARGE OFFENSIVE.)

By Maj. E. REQUIN, *General Staff, French Army.*

The hour of the assault is called:

O By English.

H By French.

All operations before and after this hour are determined in connection with the hour O or H, and with the day of attack (or day " J " in the French Army).

For example, it is foreseen in the plan of employment of the Artillery the different destructions to be executed at—

$$J—6$$
$$J—5$$
$$J—4$$
$$J—3, \text{etc.}$$

or, for the day J at:

$$6—H$$
$$5—H$$
$$½—H$$

that is to say, six, five, half an hour before the assault, and the objectives to be reached at

$$1+H$$
$$2+H$$
$$3+H$$

that is to say, one, two, three hours after the beginning of the assault.

The day " J " can be determined in advance. However, bad weather will oblige often to delay this day.

On the contrary, the hour of the general assault can be only determined on the day of the action, except if the assault is given early morning without special immediate preparation and as in consequence of the above preparation by the Artillery.

Two reasons for not determining this hour in advance:

(1) Necessity to keep the hour secret.

(2) If the assault is preceded by special preparation it is necessary:

(*a*) To know at what time after adjustment of fire the Artillery will be ready to begin the special preparation for the assault.

(*b*) To consider the time necessary to communicate the hour of the assault to all Infantry troops.

Suppose:

At 5 o'clock the Artillery commander reports:

"I am ready to begin the fire for effect."
The duration of this fire must be half an hour.
The necessary time to communicate to Infantry is 2½ hours.
The assault can be given at H+5+2½ H=7½ H and the special preparation by Artillery will begin at 7 o'clock.
The communication to the Infantry will be:

$$H = 7½ H.$$

It is right to add that the *tendency in large offensives* is now to determine in advance (when possible) the hour of the general assault. Three reasons:

1. The duration and efficiency of the above preparation by Artillery fire required to complete the necessary damage or destruction before the day of the general attack. Therefore the immediate preparation by fire is less important and can be *sometimes* omitted.

2. The best Artillery officers certify that it is possible and advisable instead to readjust the fire on the day of the attack by making meteorological observations and changes in firing data on that account only, to correct the bridge of the day before.

3. With large units deployed for the battle it takes a long time to communicate an order to Infantry units (about 6 hours).

The above is an example of the continual changes in methods; not in principle, of course, but in the methods employed in this war. However, the *rule* to be observed remains as follows:

(*a*) Not to begin Artillery fire for effect before obtaining the bridge by one means or another.

(*b*) Not to deliver the general assault before—

(1) The necessary destruction has been completed by Artillery fire.

(2) The necessary time has elapsed so that all *Infantry units* can receive notice of the *precise hour* of the assault.

○